Six String
Music Journal

I0487953

By
The
Playful
Geeks

We hate putting this stuff here but the publisher says we have to.

Date:

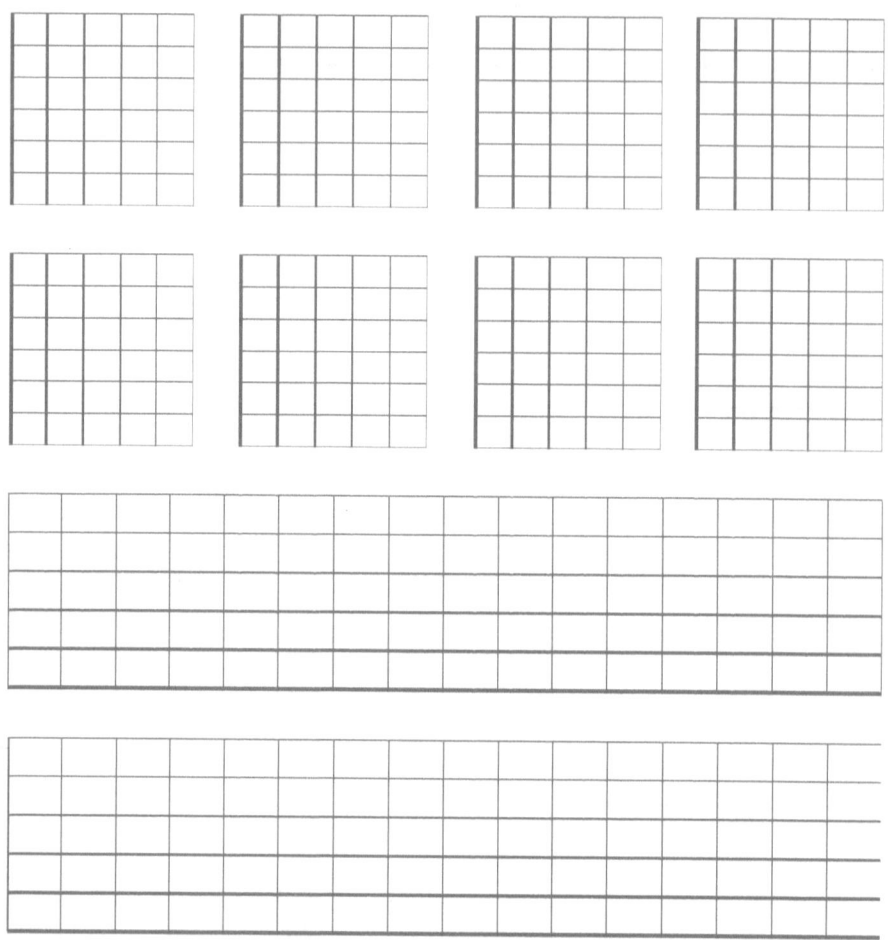

Notes

TAB

TAB

TAB

Date:

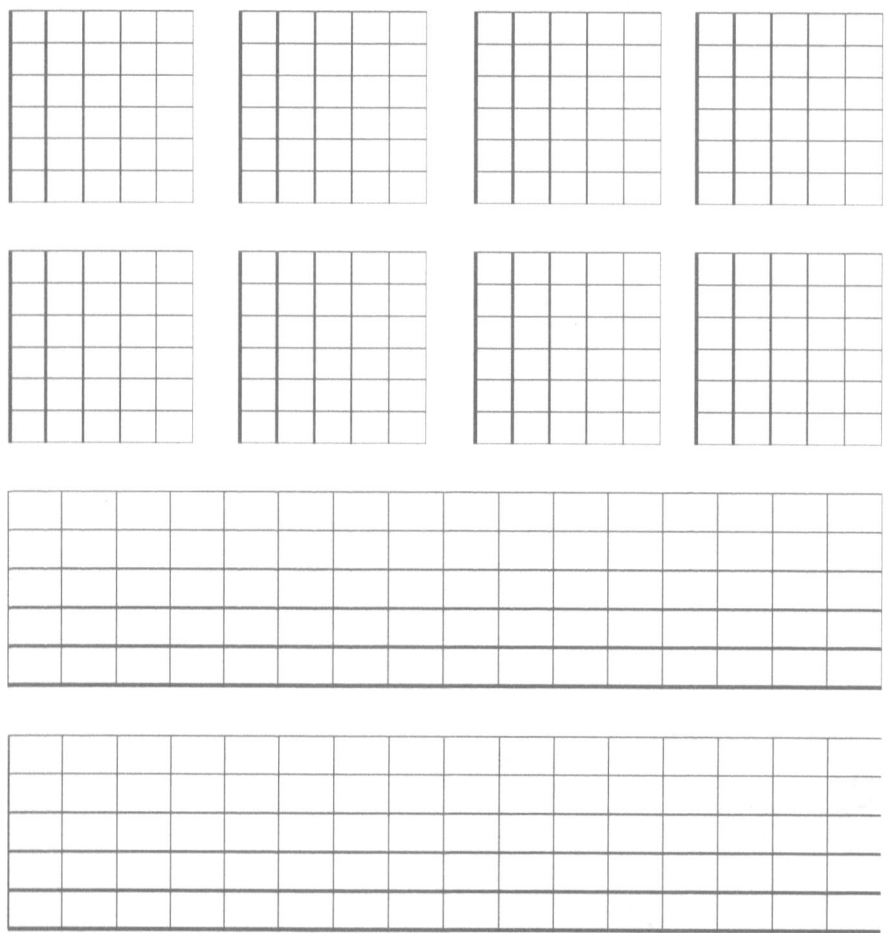

Notes

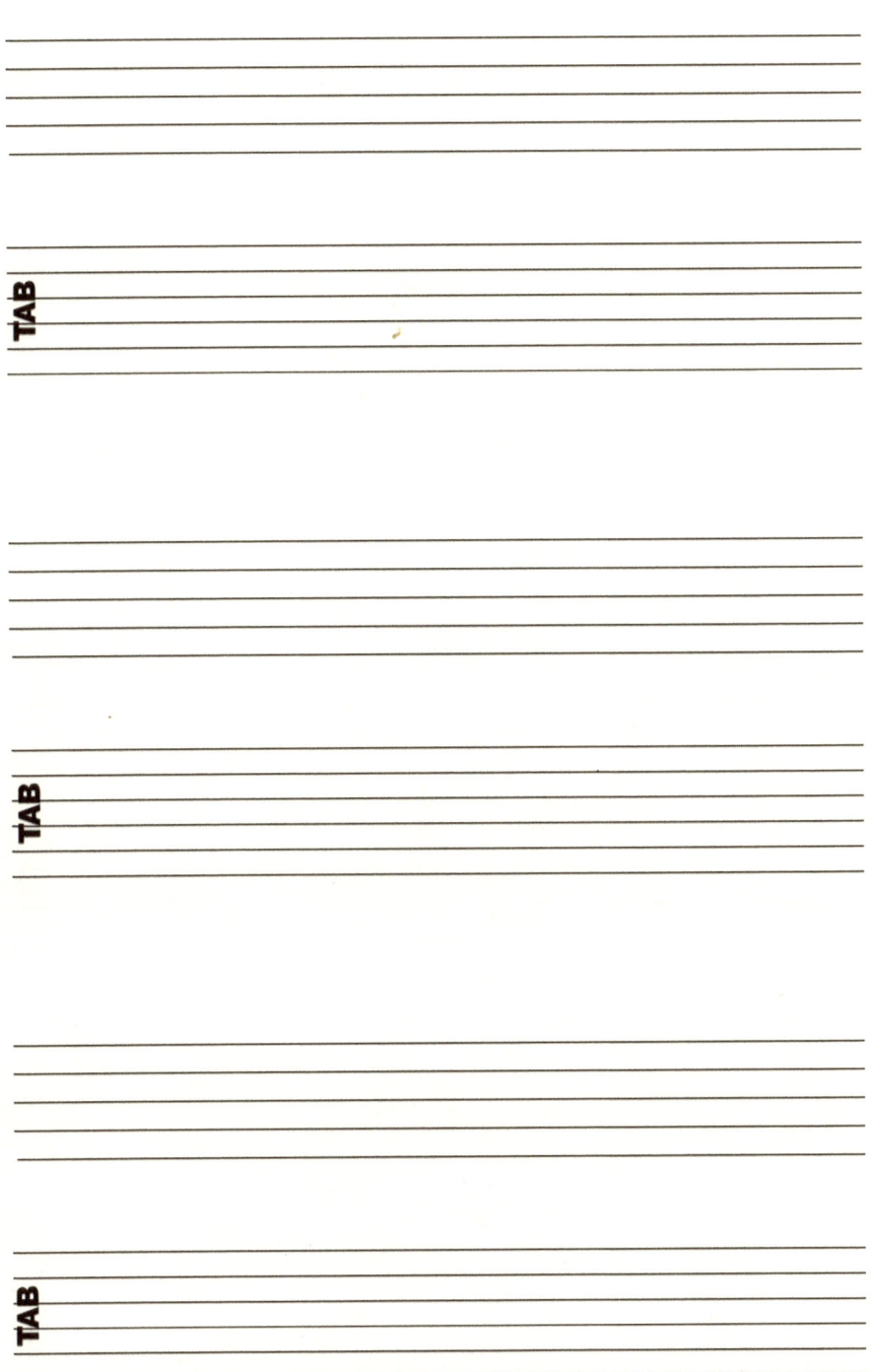

Date:

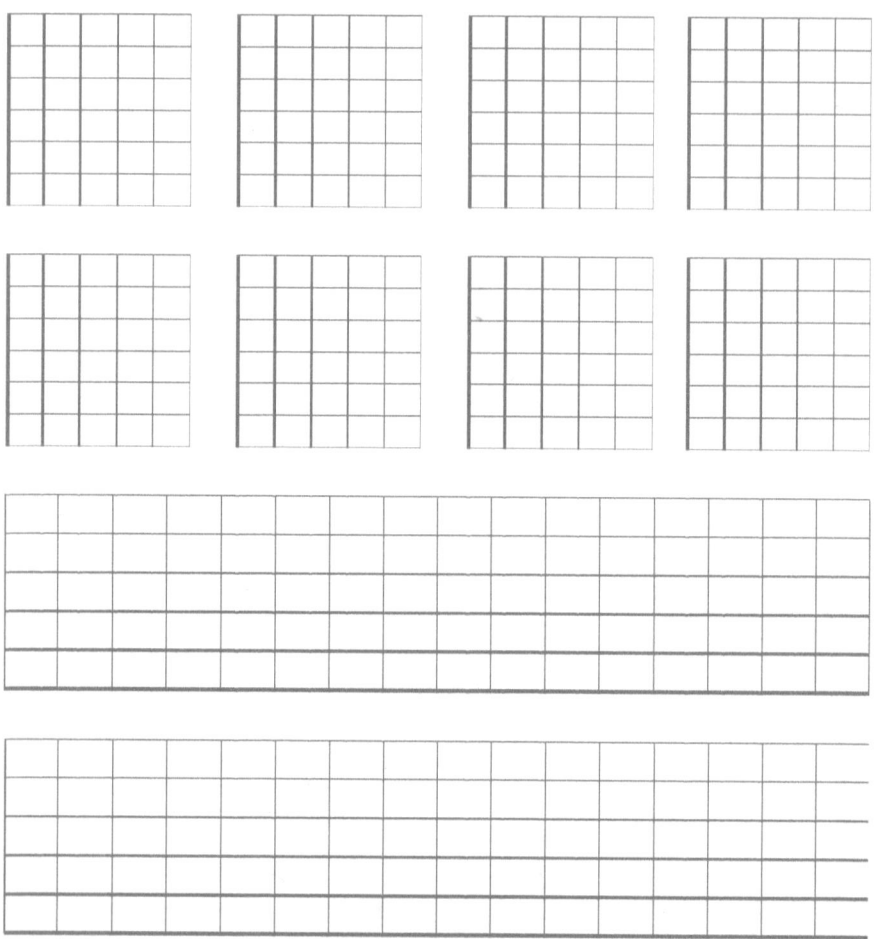

Notes

TAB

TAB

TAB

Date:

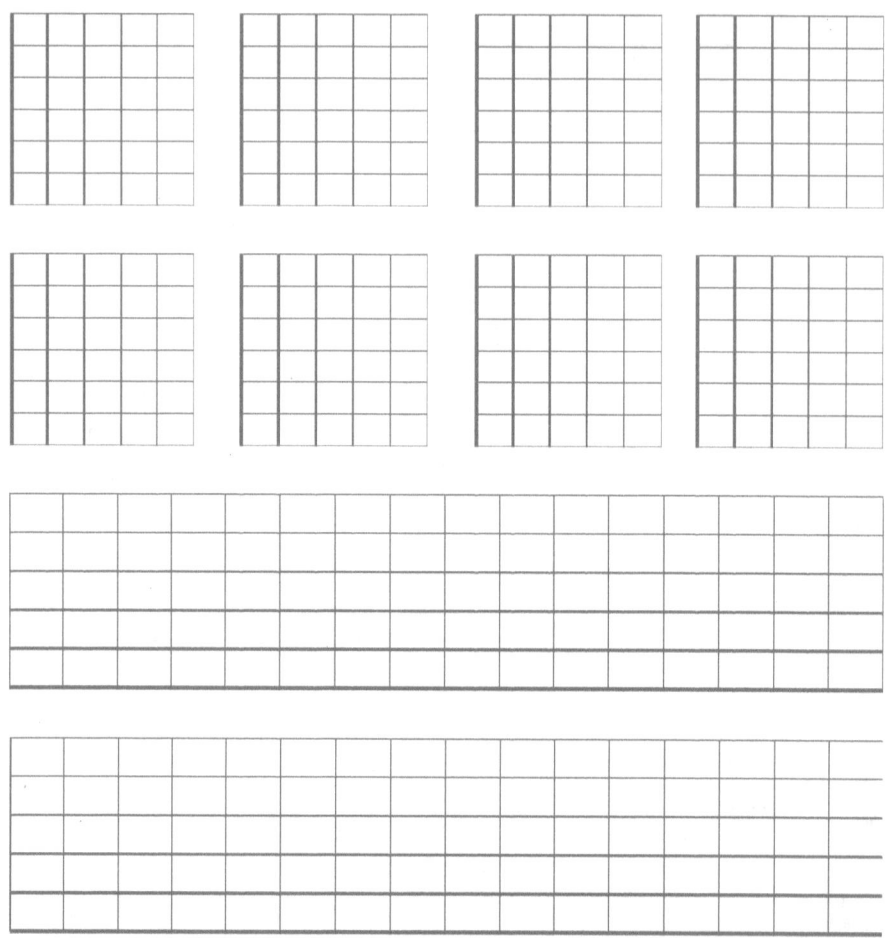

Notes

TAB

TAB

TAB

Date:

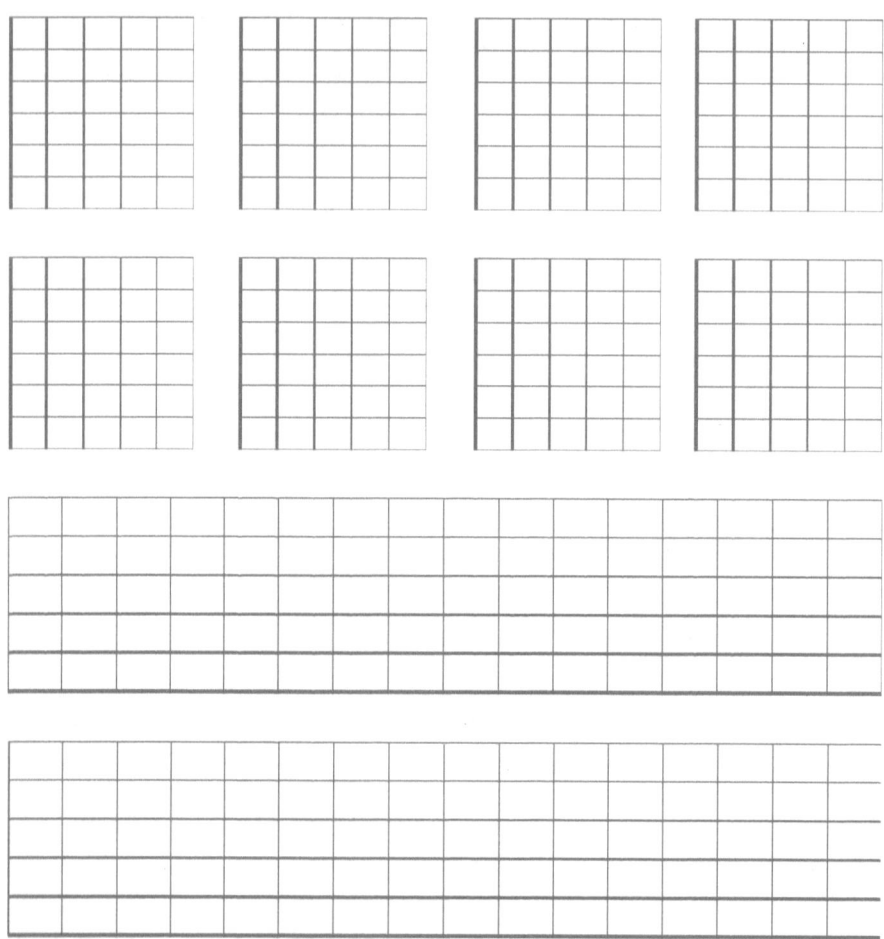

Notes

TAB

TAB

TAB

Date:

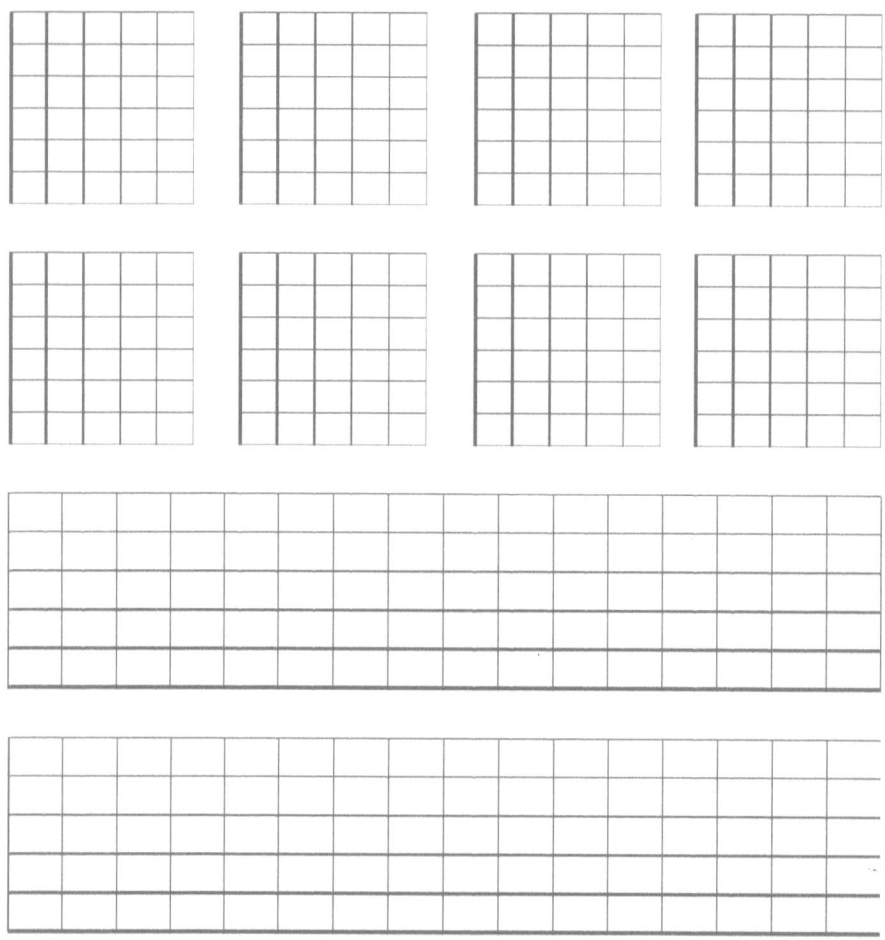

Notes

TAB

TAB

TAB

Date:

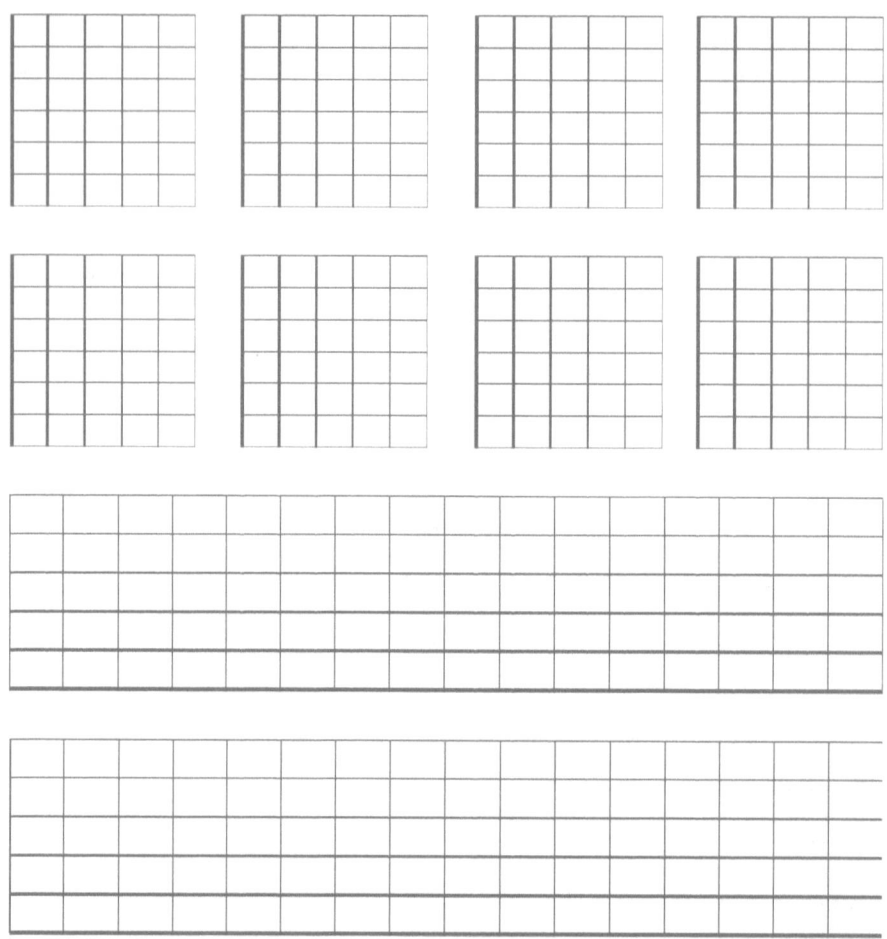

Notes

TAB

TAB

TAB

Date:

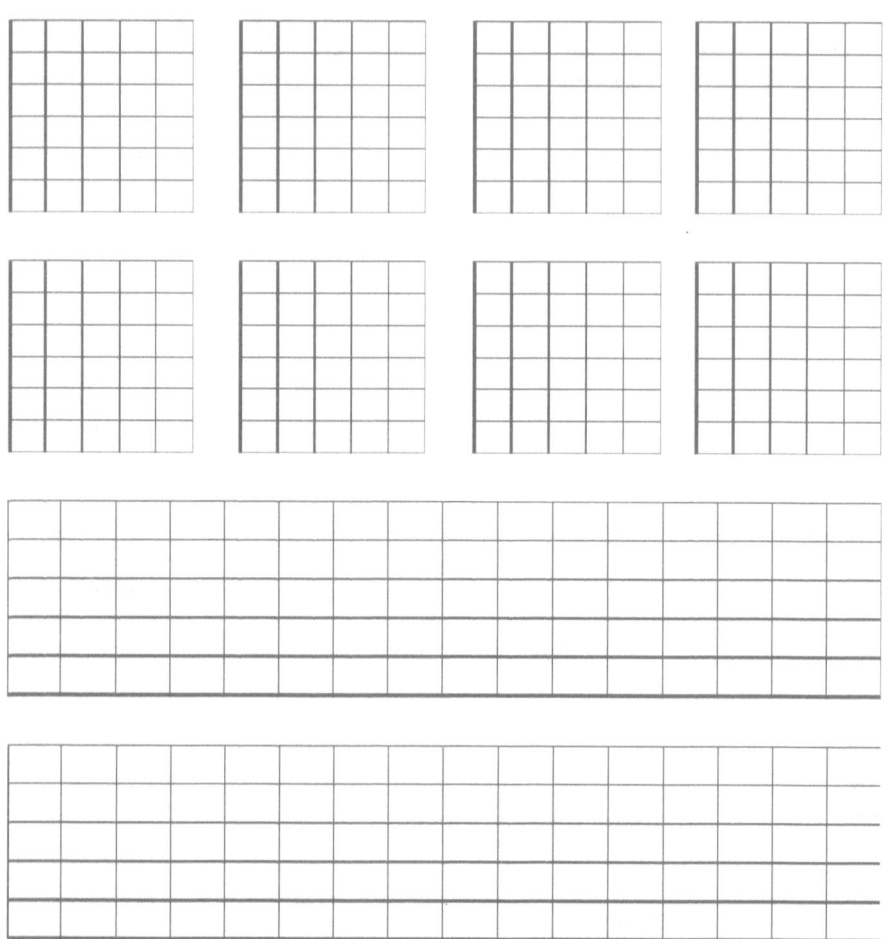

Notes

TAB

TAB

TAB

Date:

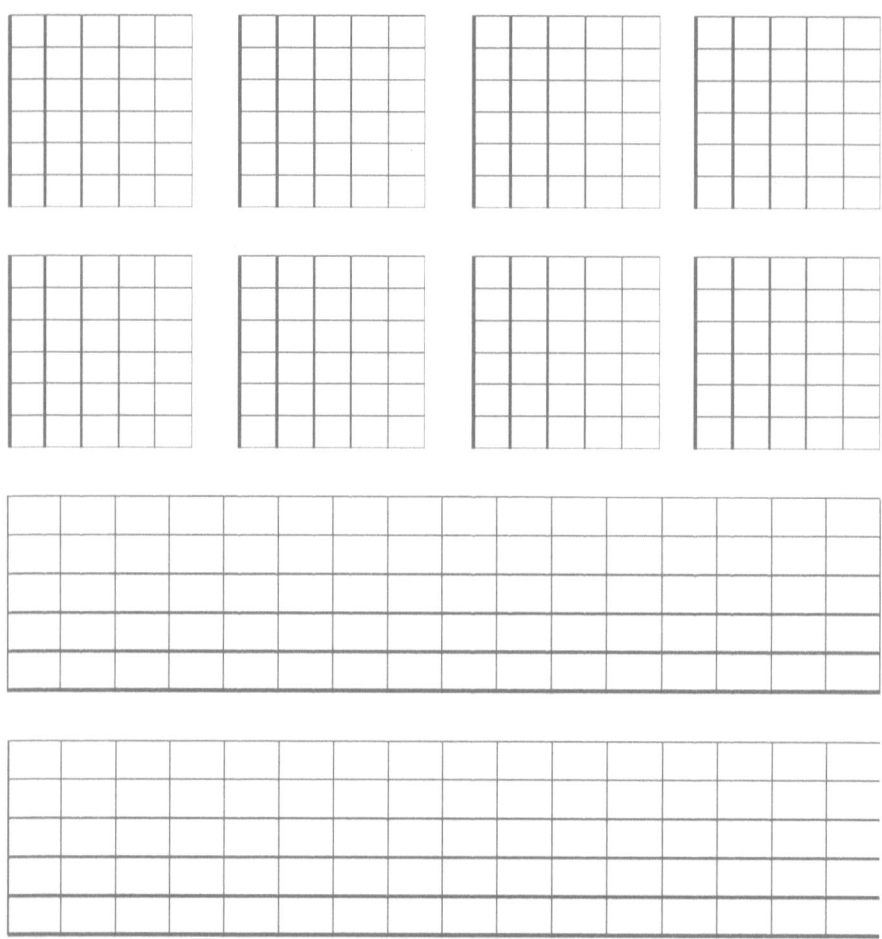

Notes

TAB

TAB

TAB

Date:

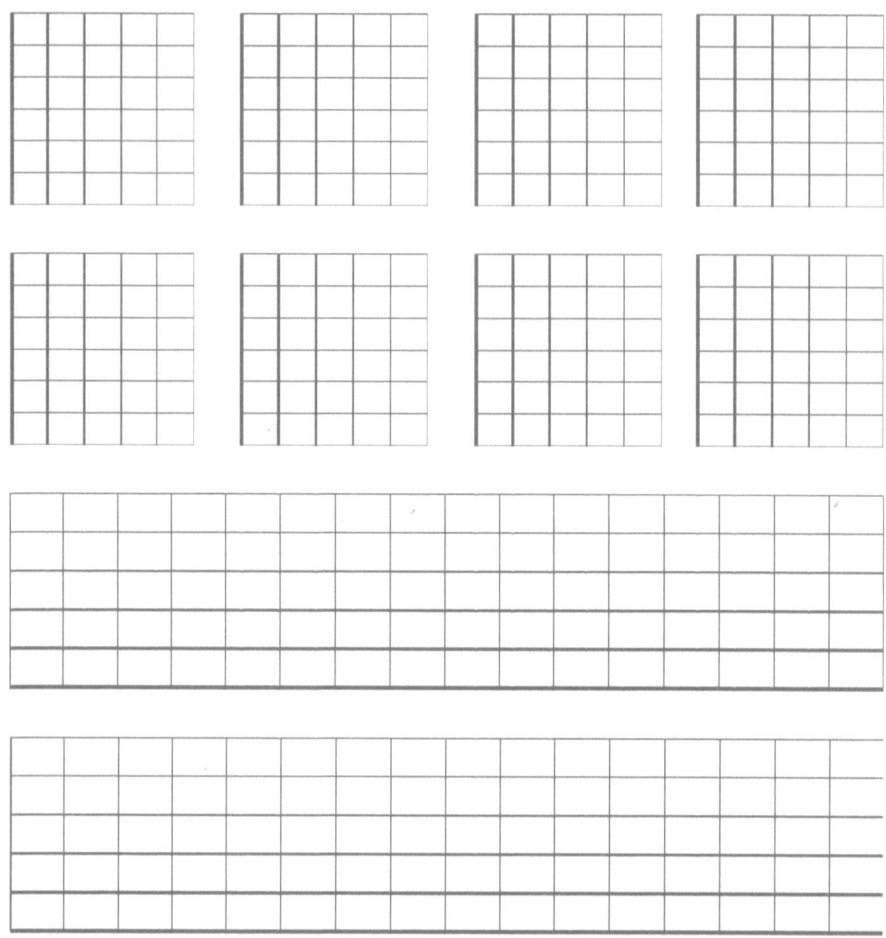

Notes

TAB

TAB

TAB

Date:

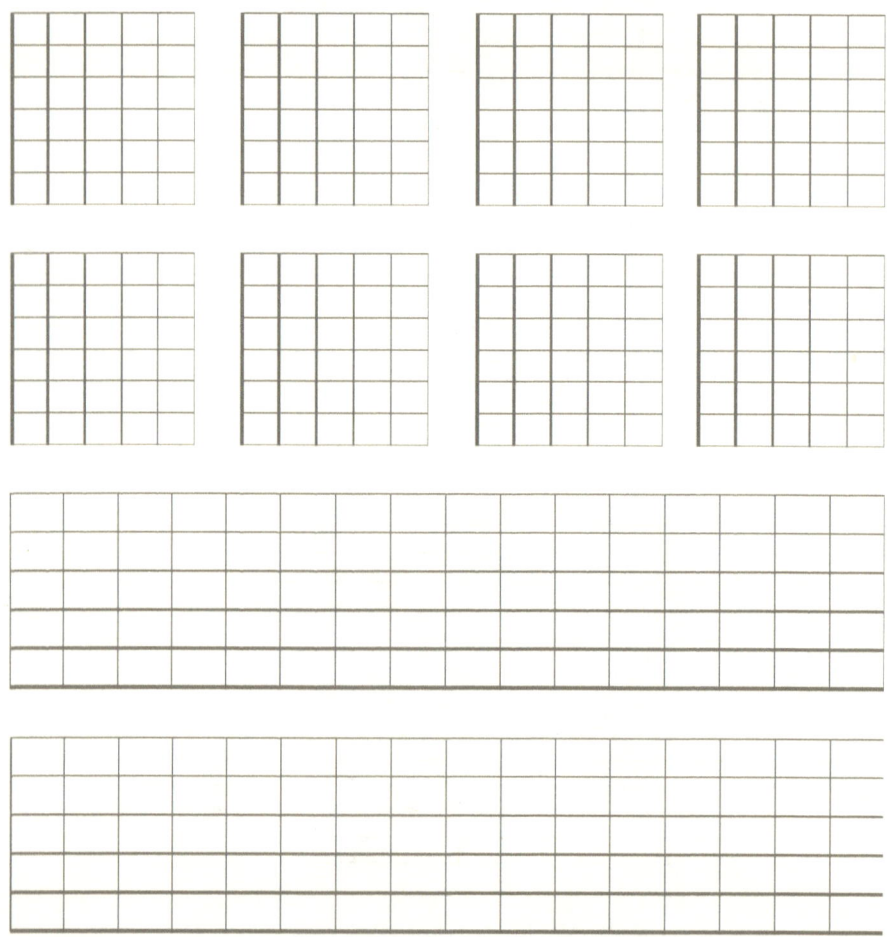

Notes

TAB

TAB

TAB

Date:

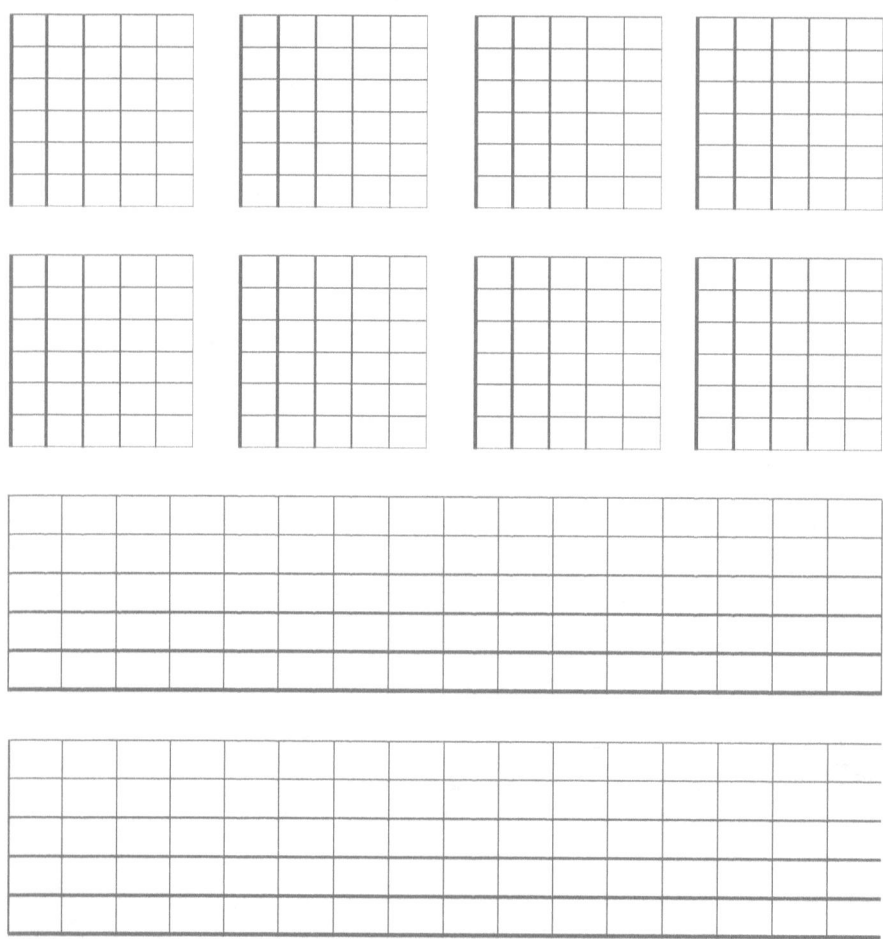

Notes

TAB

TAB

TAB

Date:

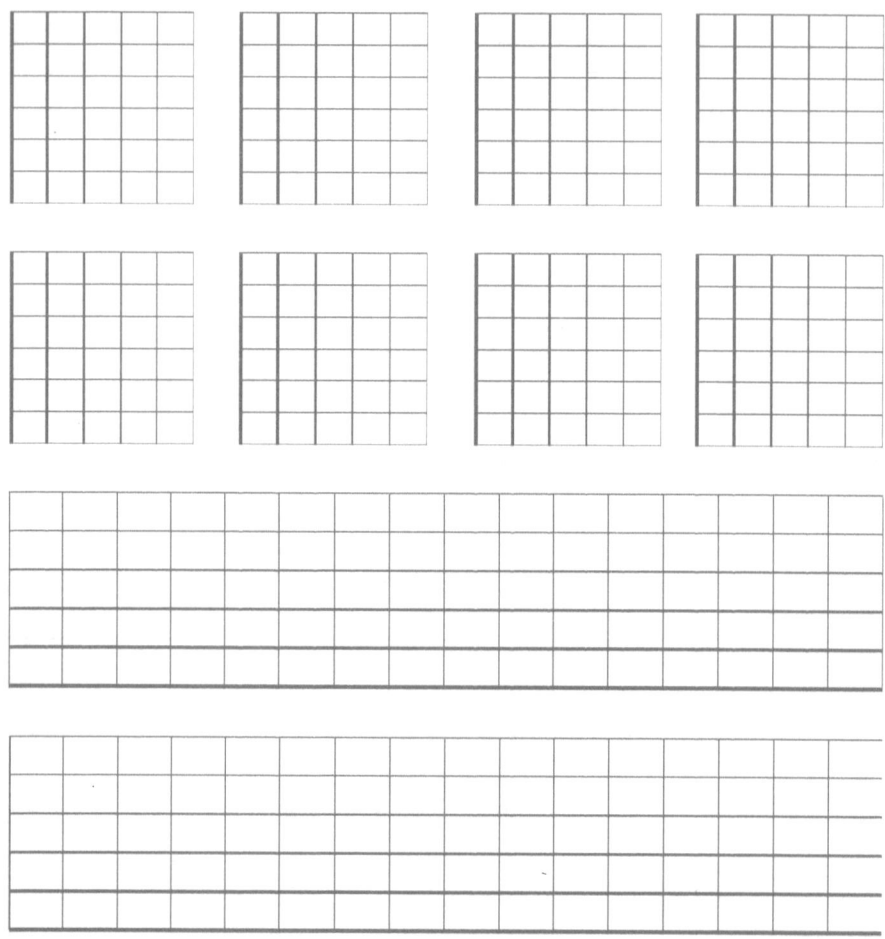

Notes

TAB

TAB

TAB

Date:

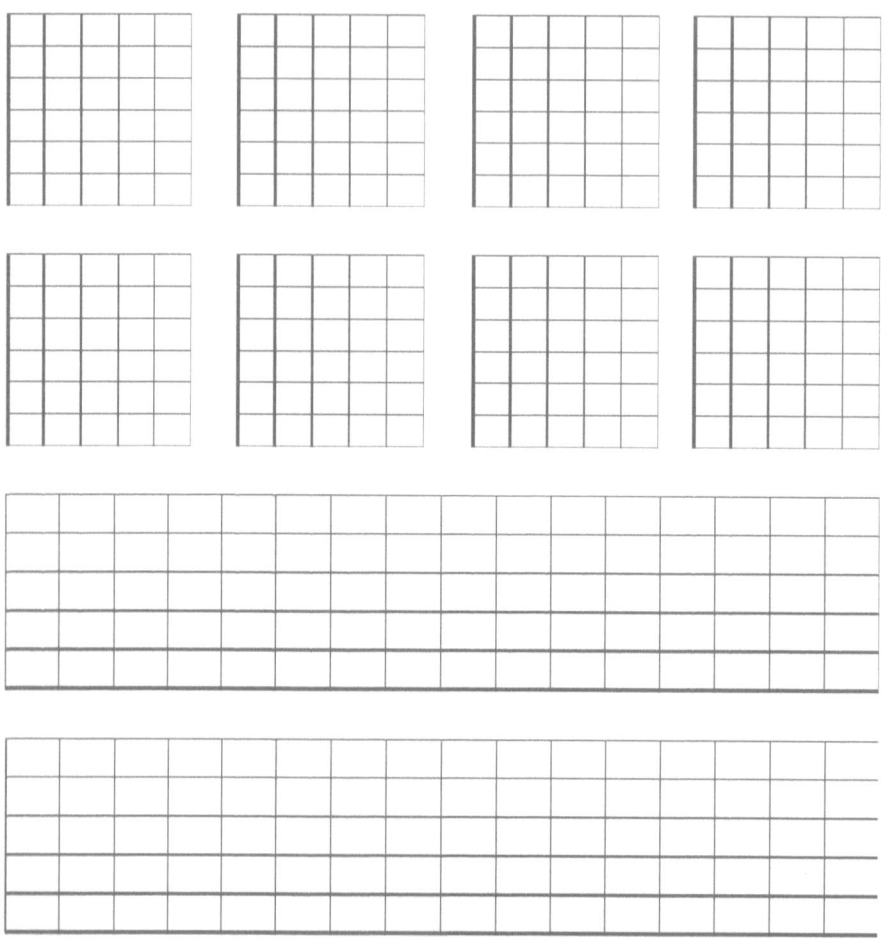

Notes

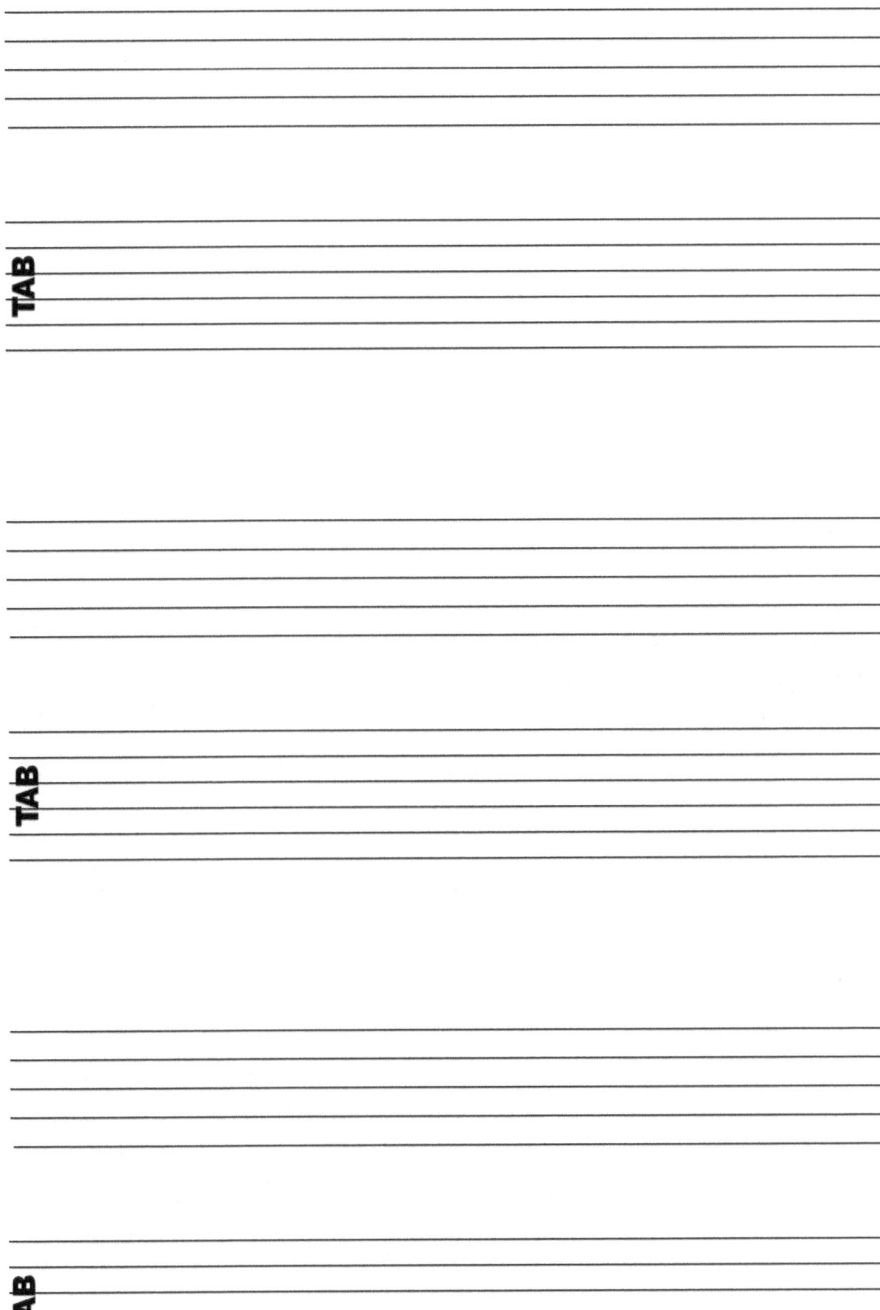

Date:

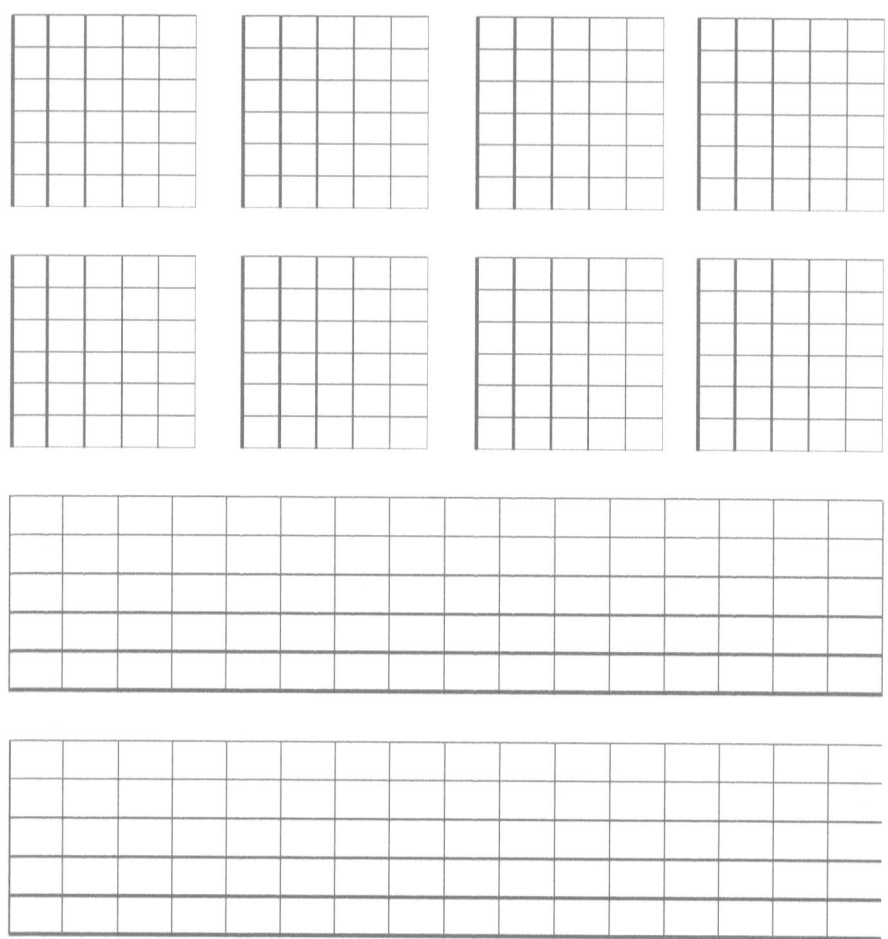

Notes

TAB

TAB

TAB

Date:

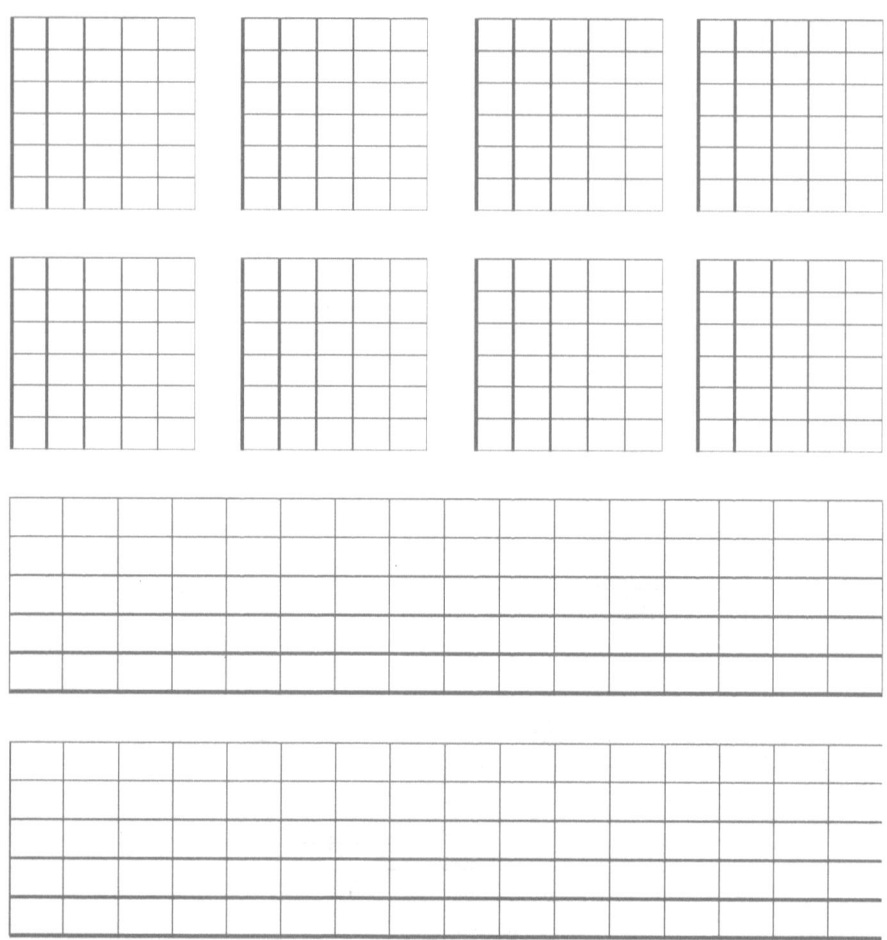

Notes

TAB

TAB

TAB

Date:

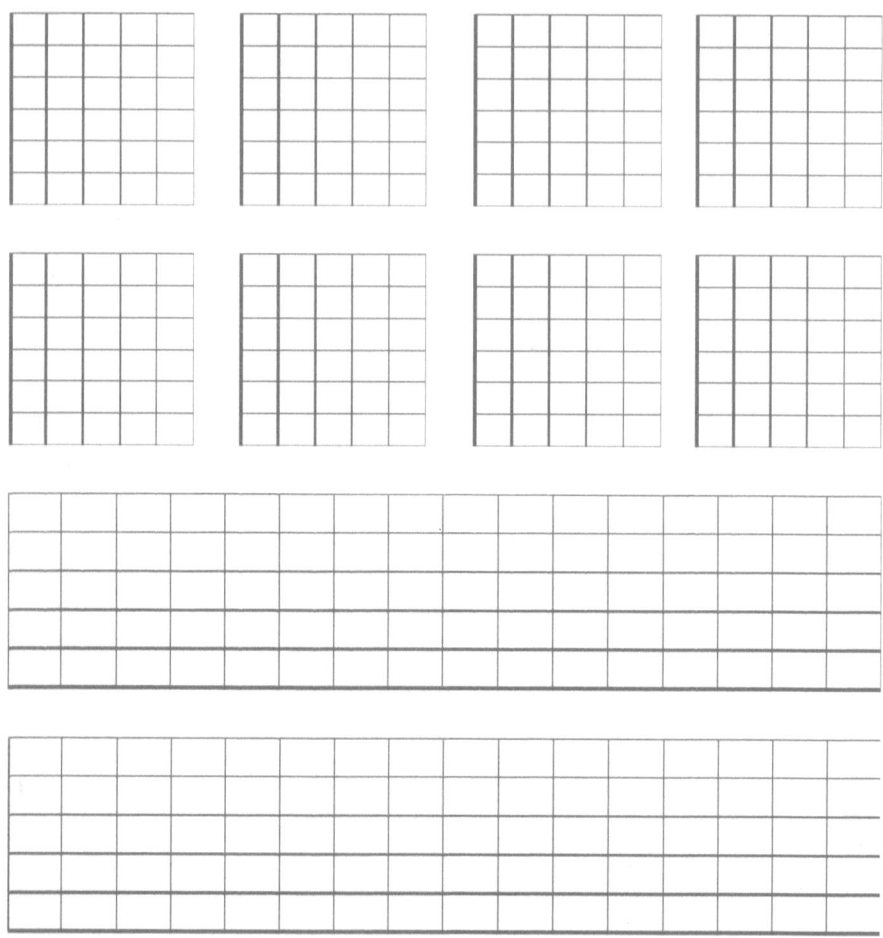

Notes

TAB

TAB

TAB

Date:

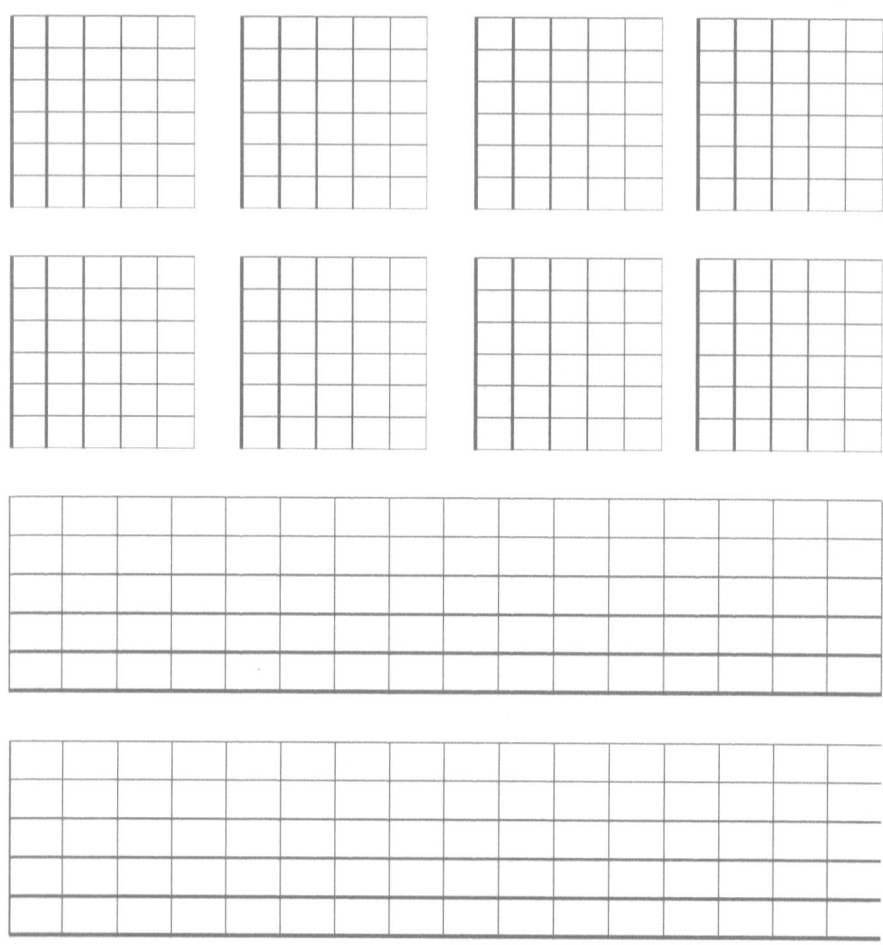

Notes

TAB

TAB

TAB

Date:

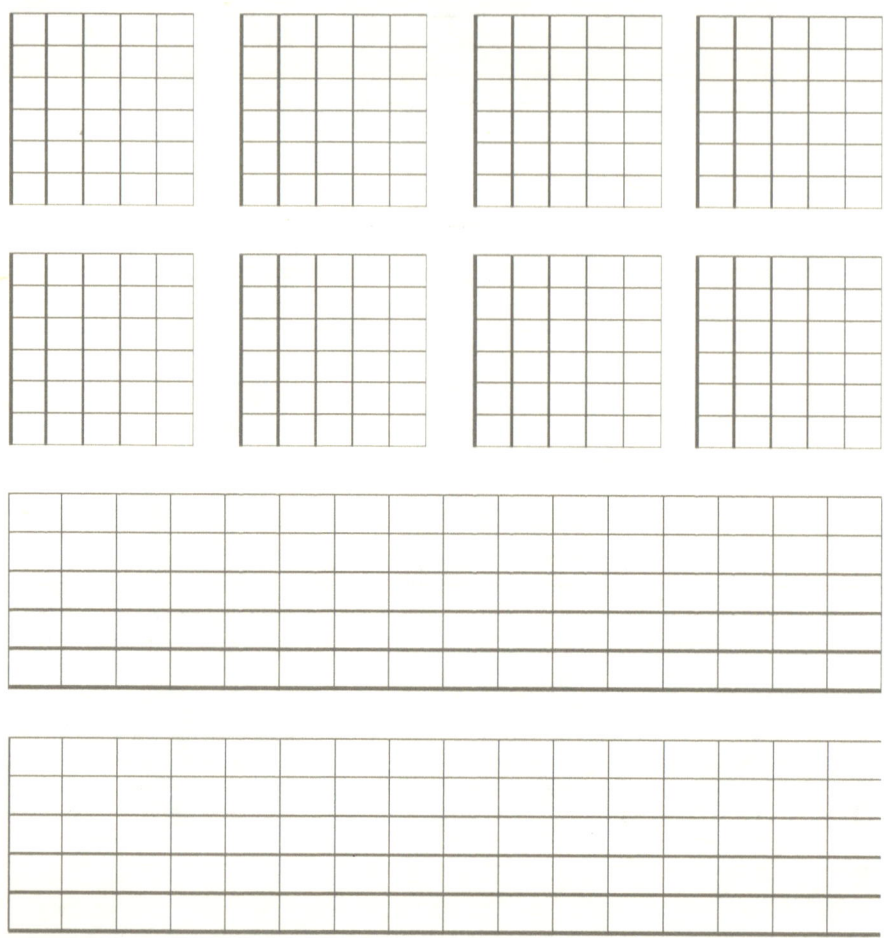

Notes

TAB

TAB

TAB

Date:

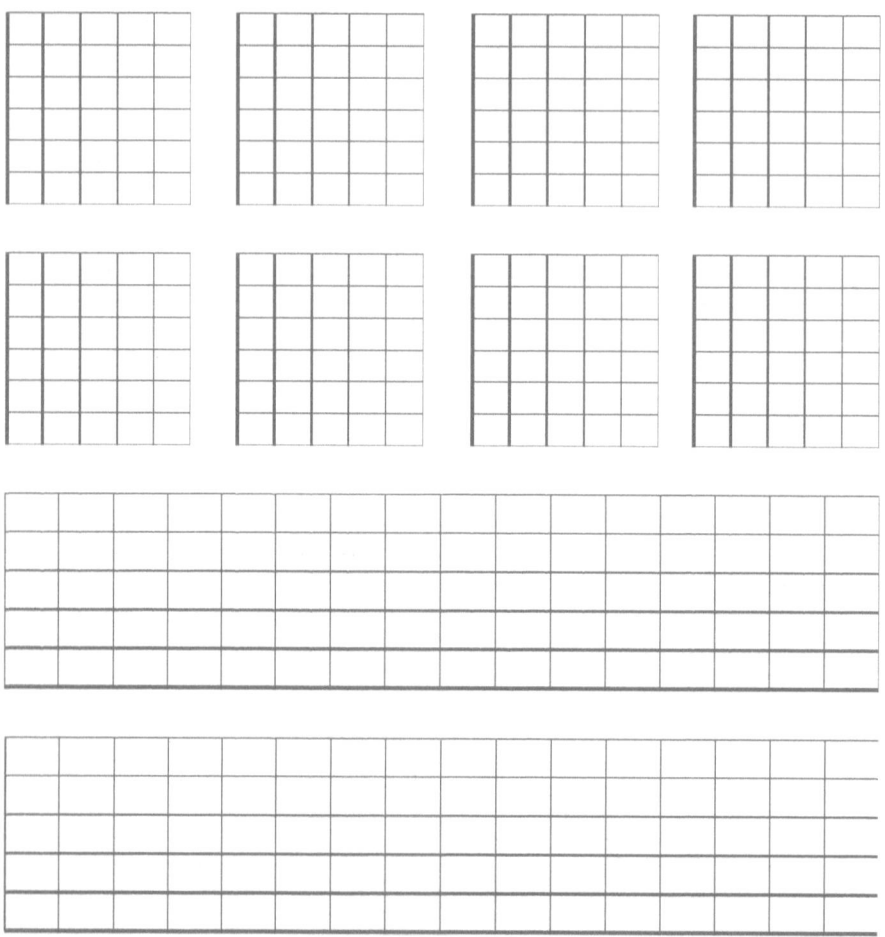

Notes

TAB

TAB

TAB

Date:

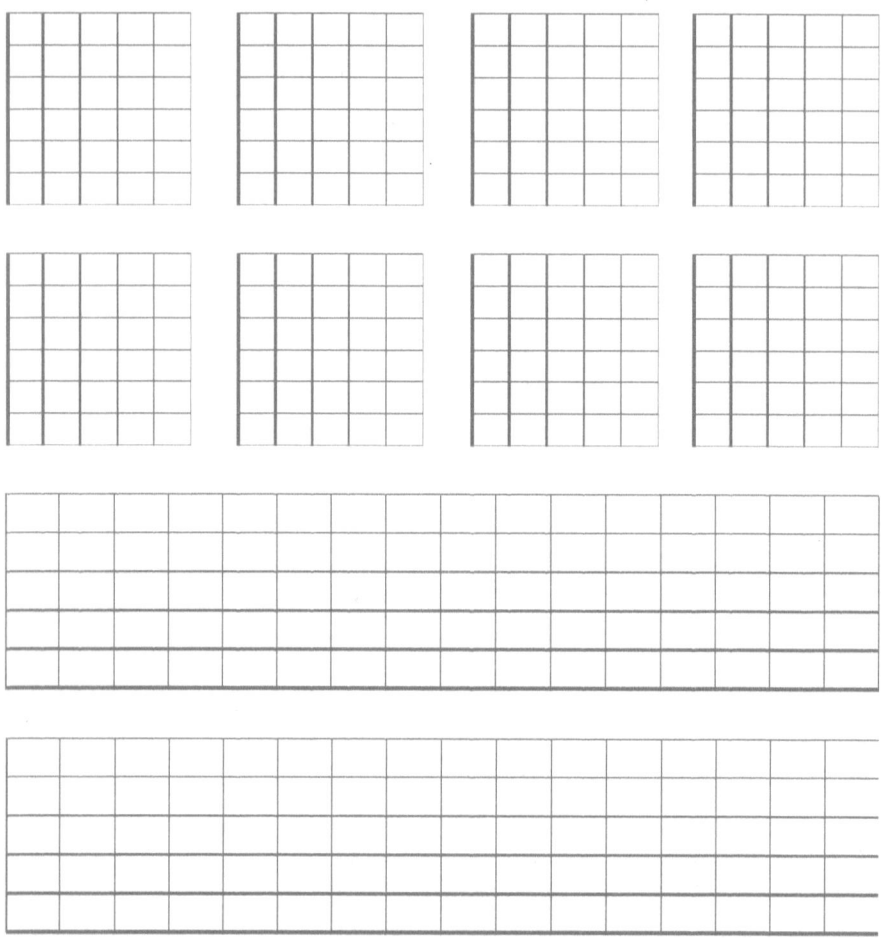

Notes

TAB

TAB

TAB

Date:

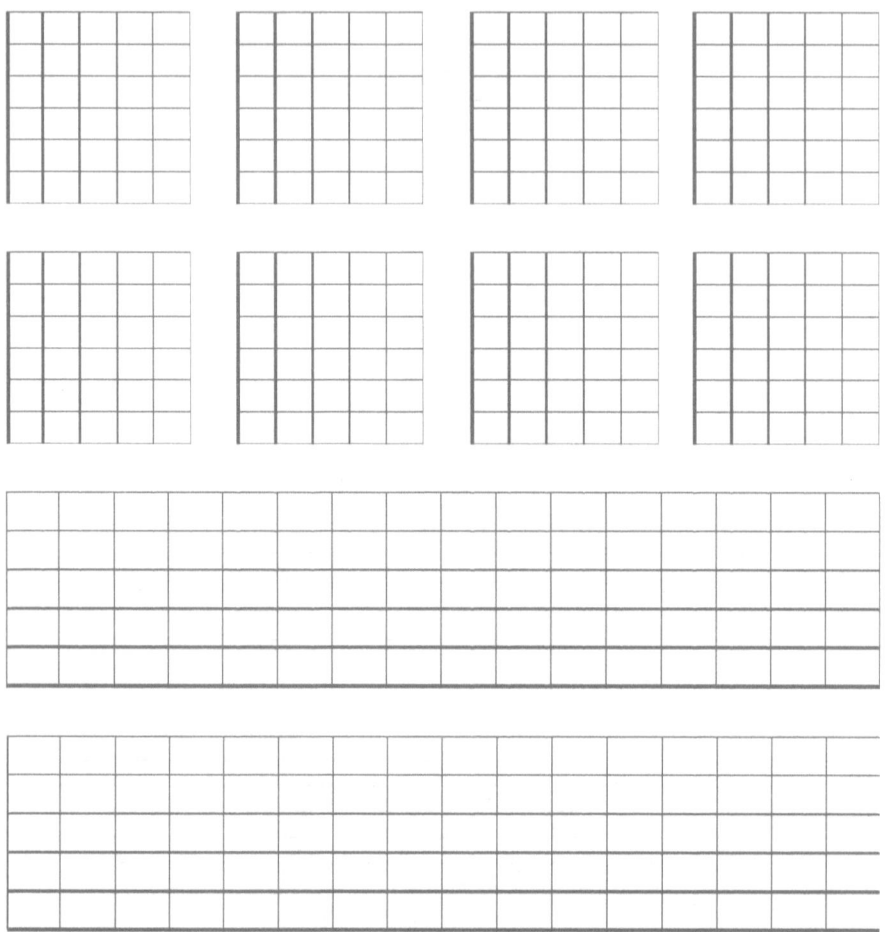

Notes

TAB

TAB

TAB

Date:

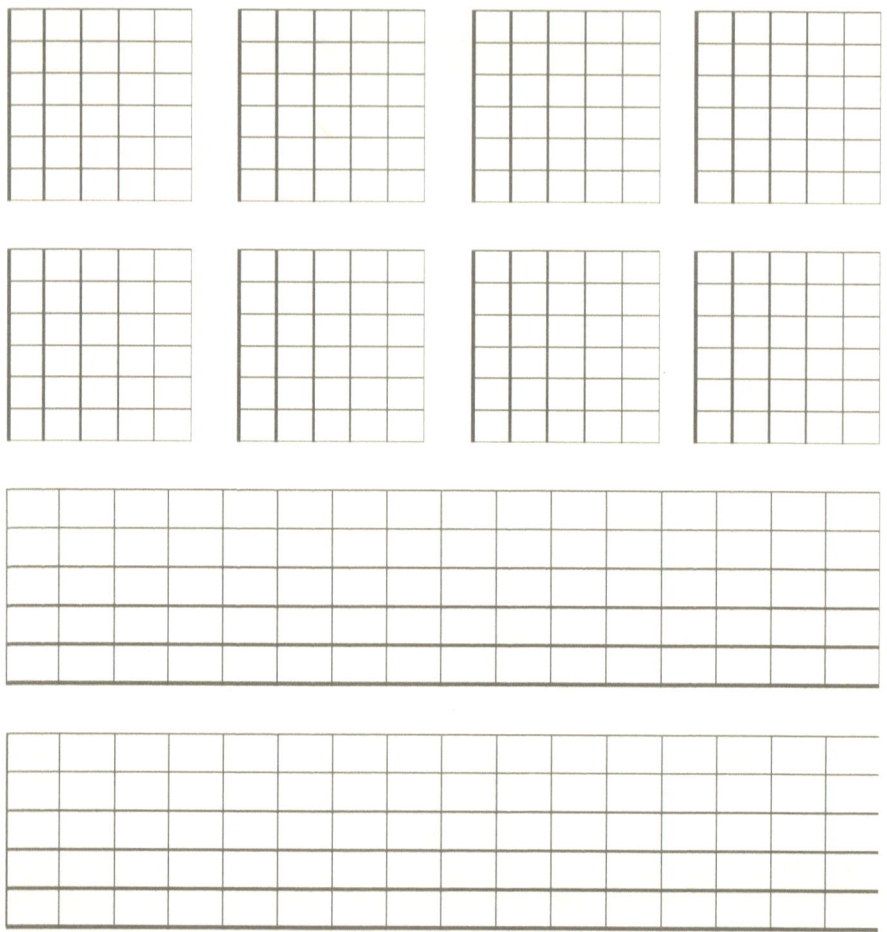

Notes

TAB

TAB

TAB

Date:

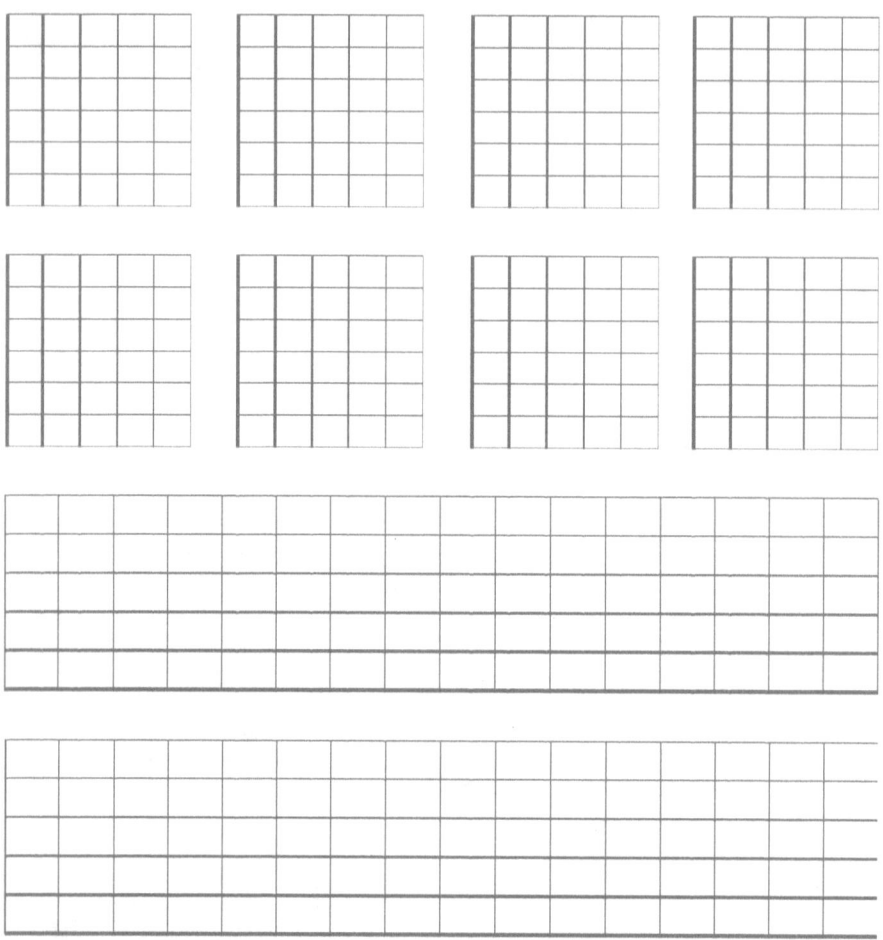

Notes

TAB

TAB

TAB

Date:

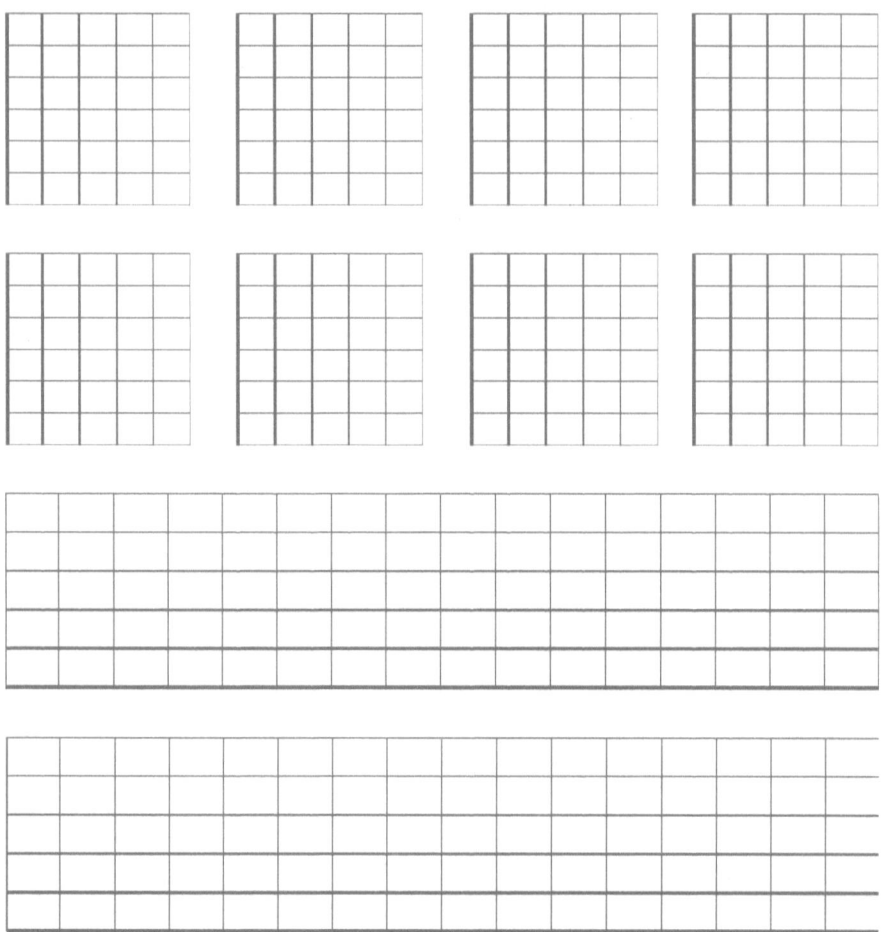

Notes

TAB

TAB

TAB

Date:

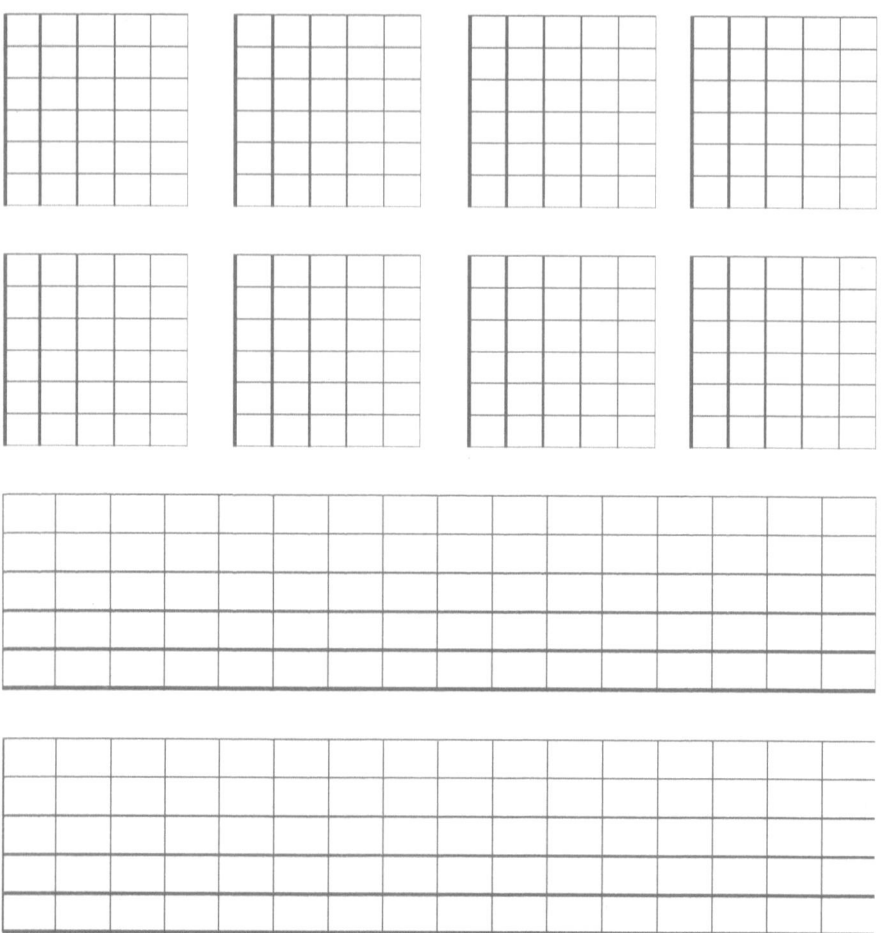

Notes

TAB

TAB

TAB

Date:

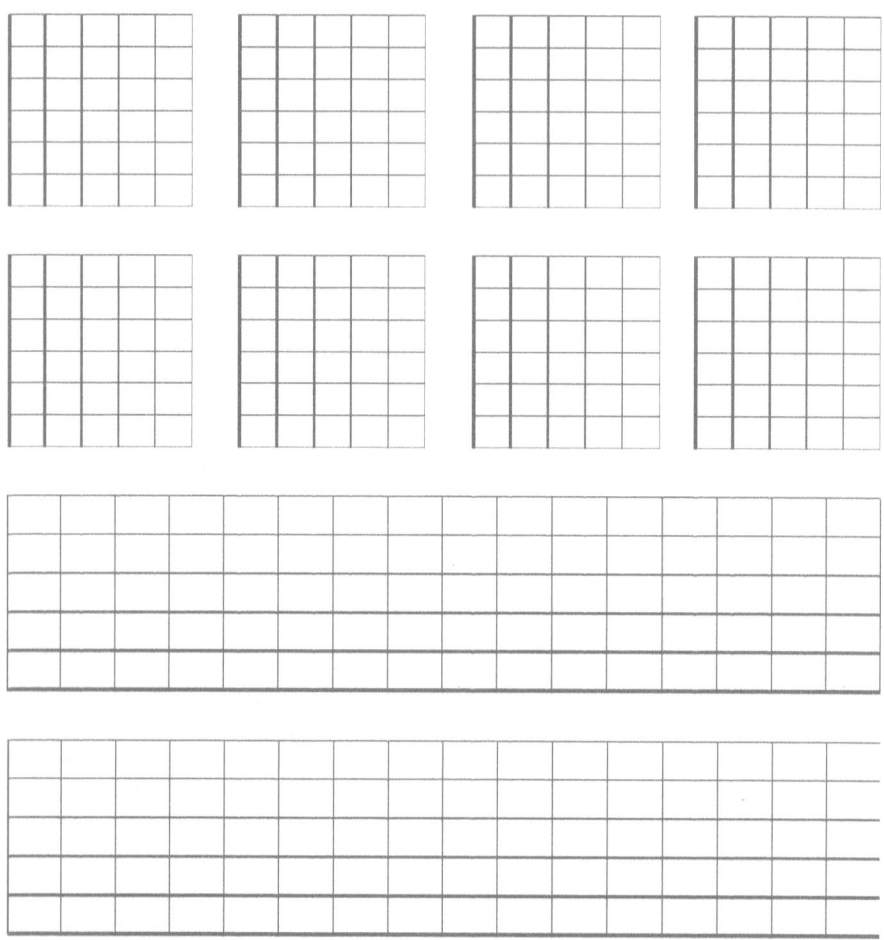

Notes

TAB

TAB

TAB

Date:

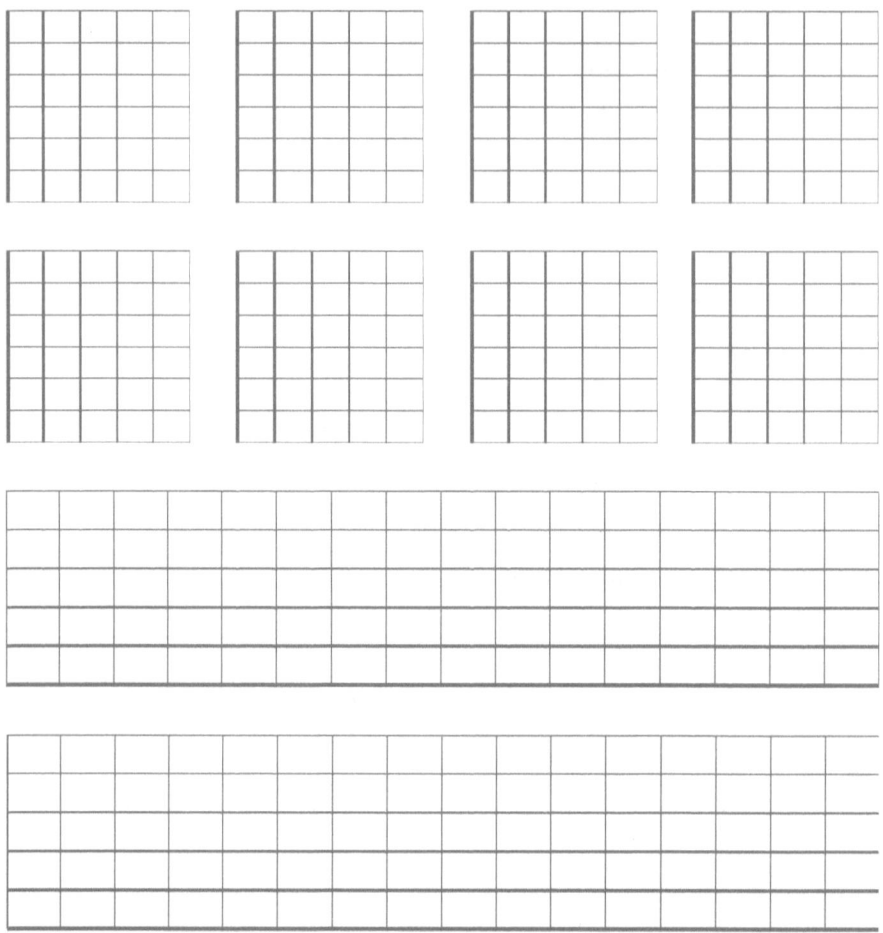

Notes

TAB

TAB

TAB

Date:

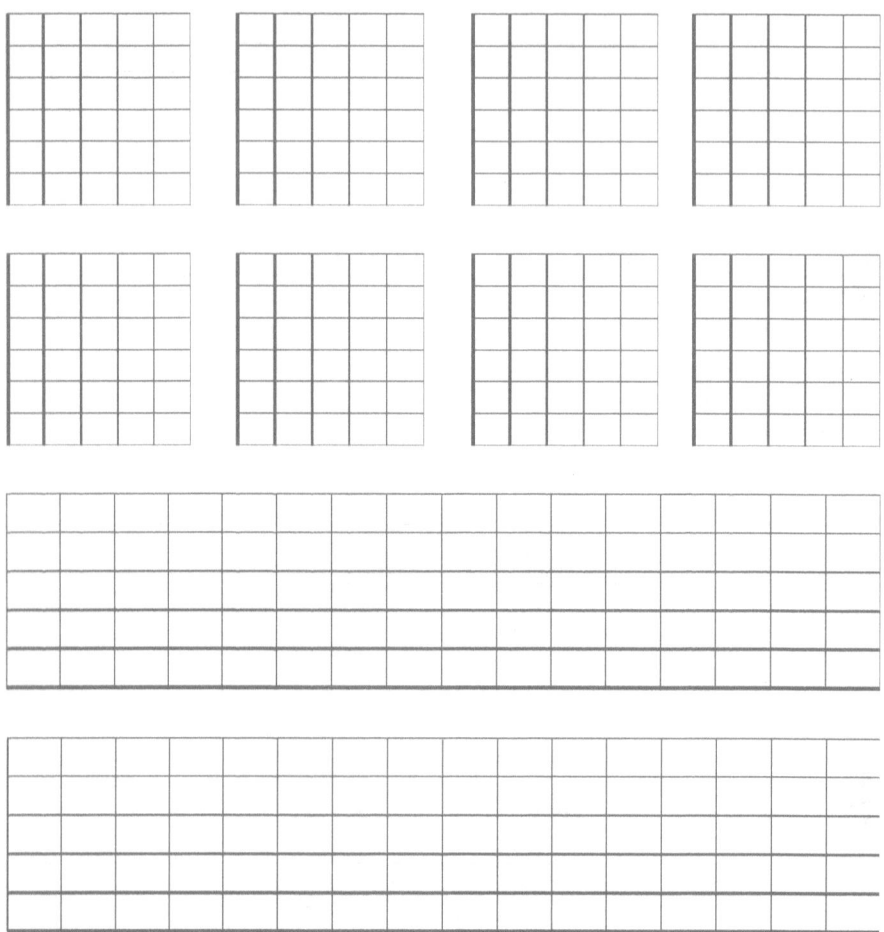

Notes

TAB

TAB

TAB

Date:

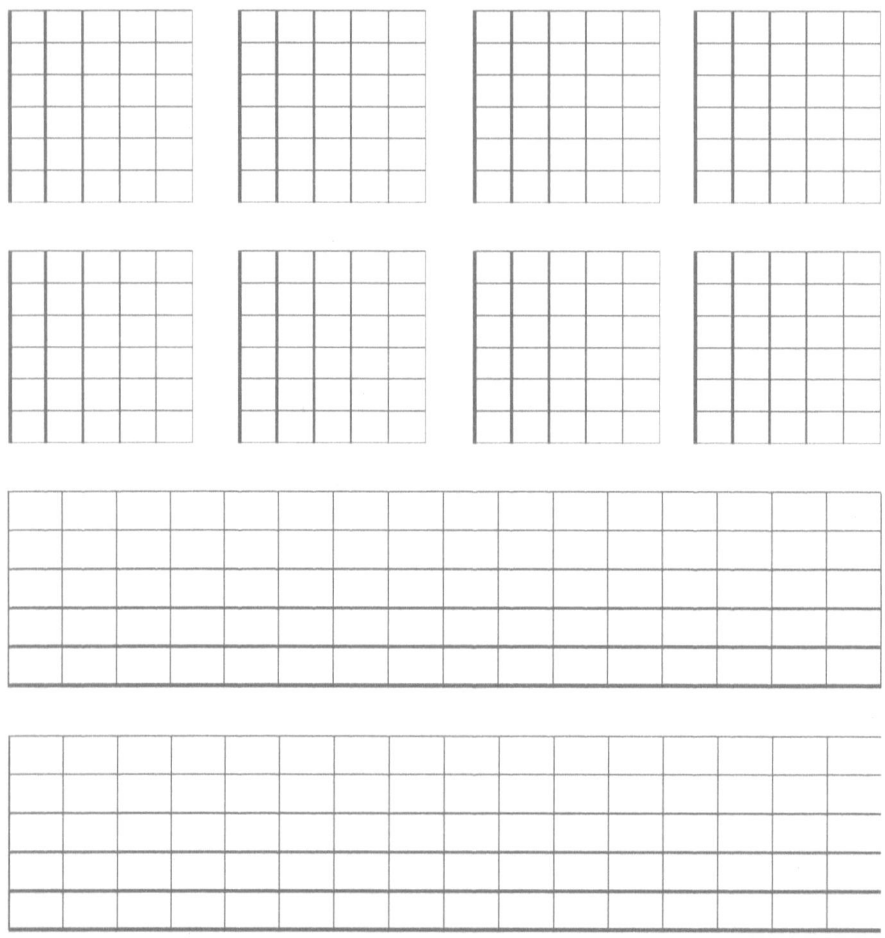

Notes

TAB

TAB

TAB

Date:

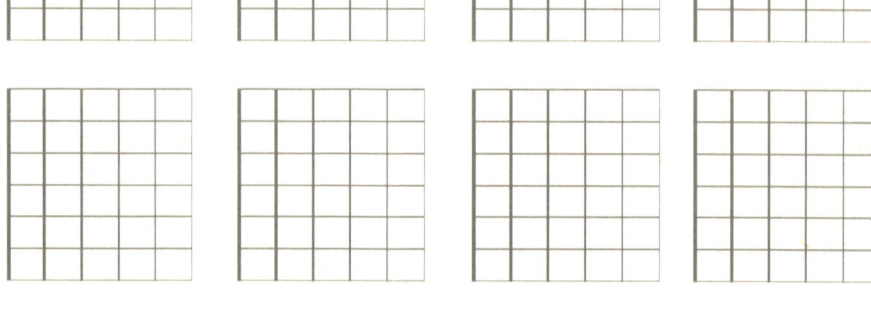

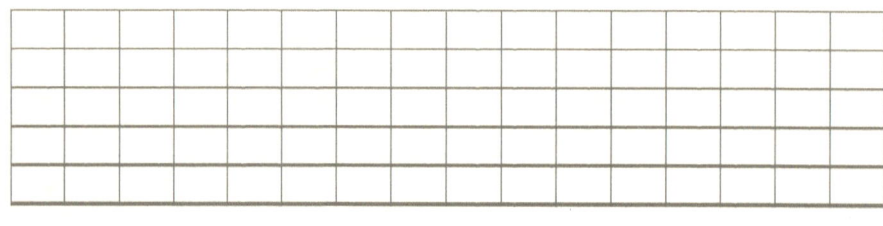

Notes

TAB

TAB

TAB

Date:

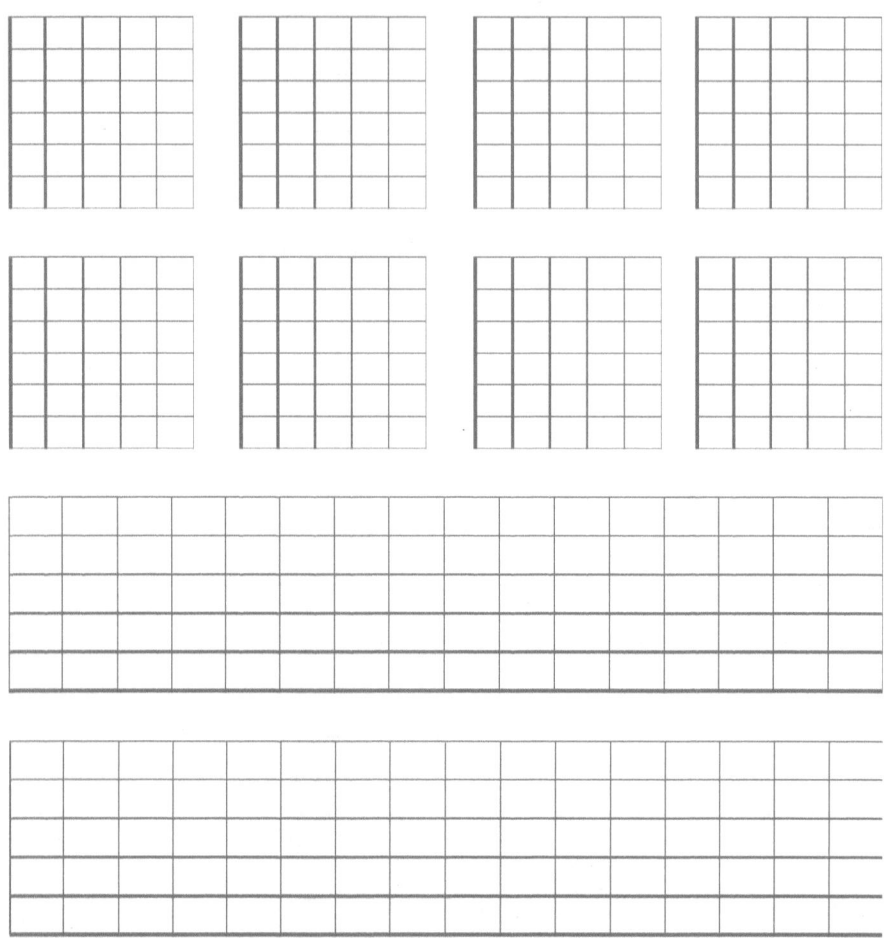

Notes

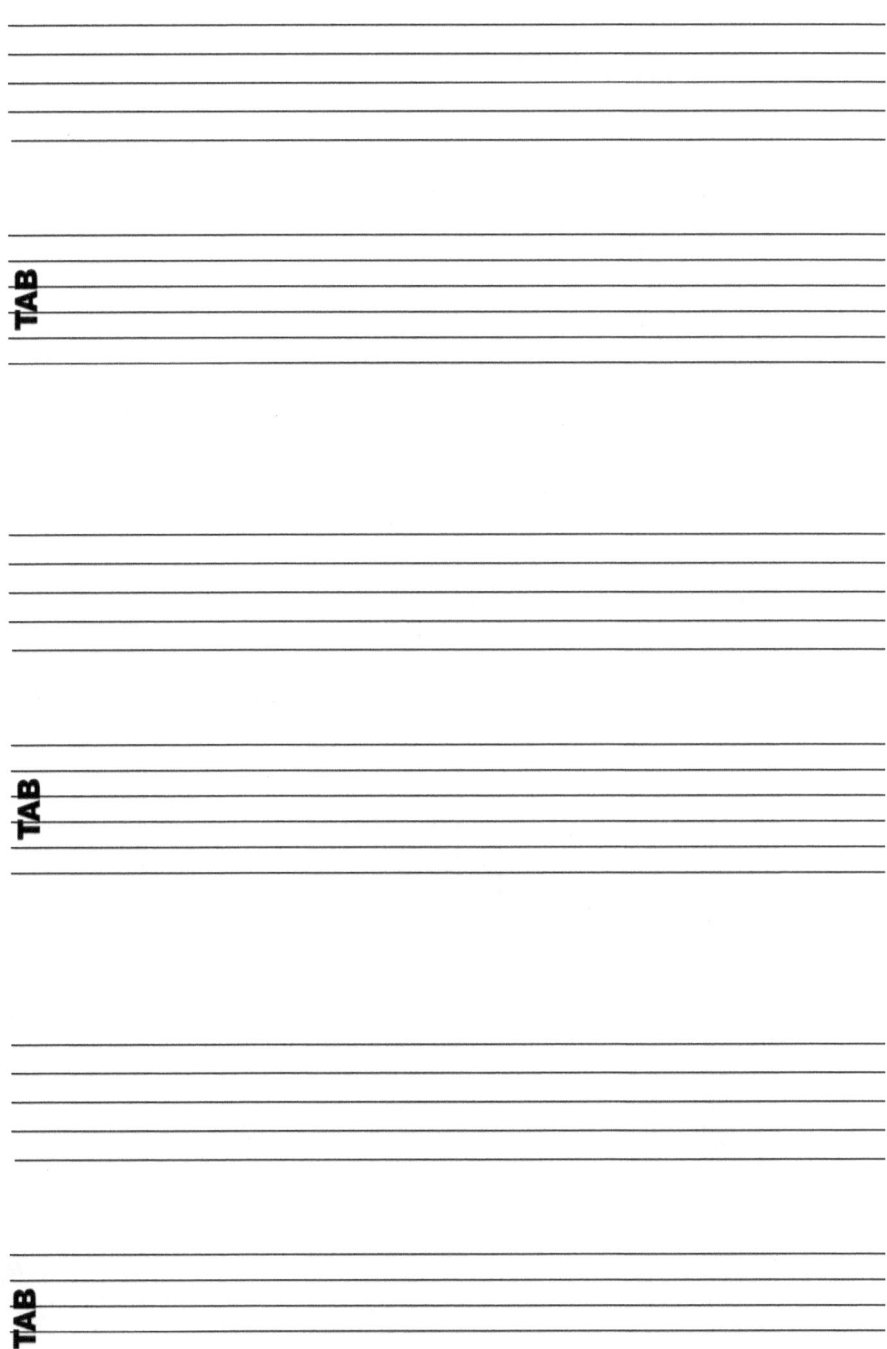

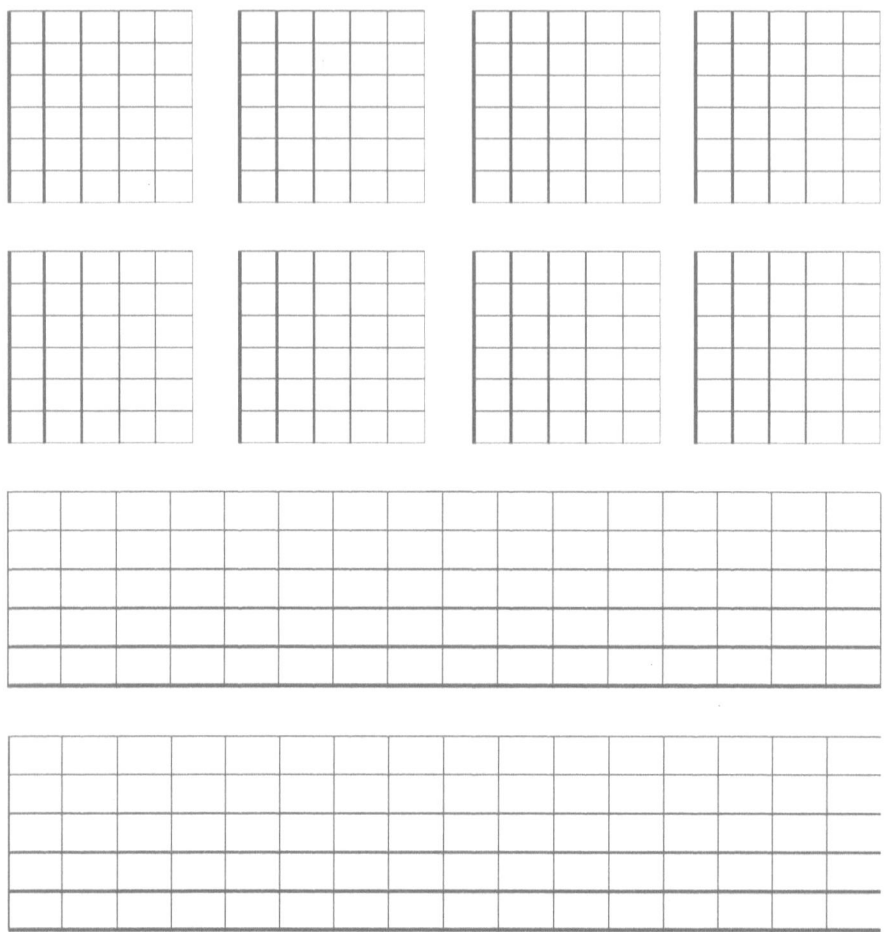

TAB

TAB

TAB

Date:

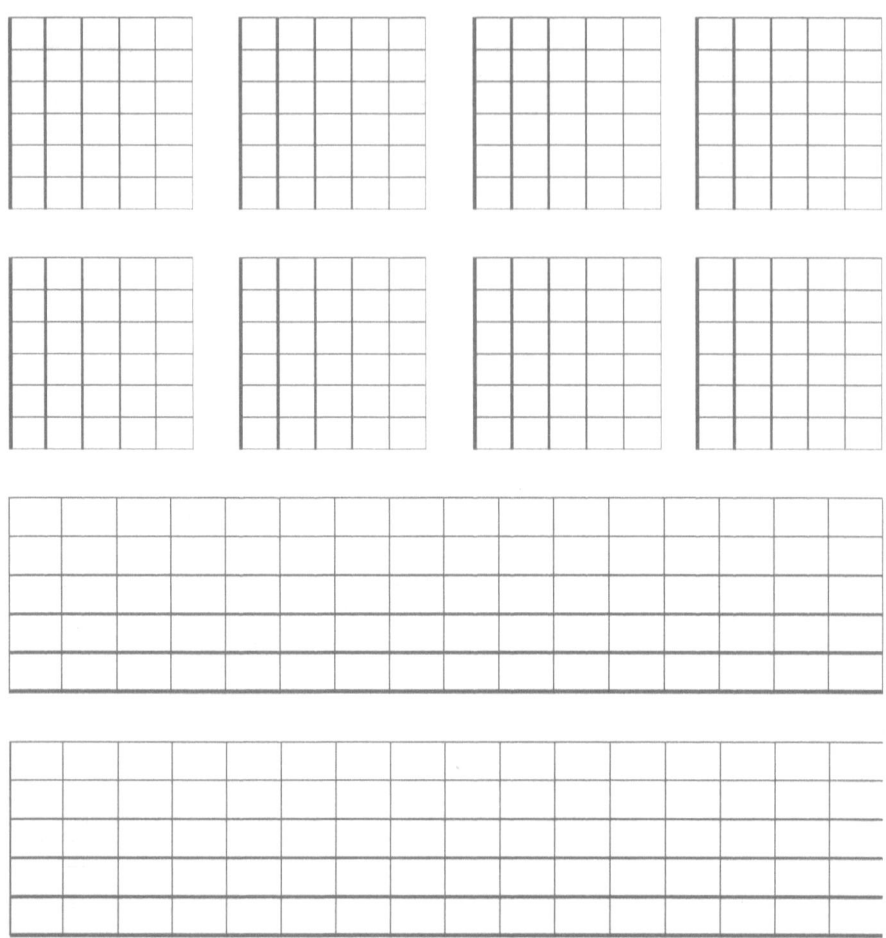

Notes

TAB

TAB

TAB

Date:

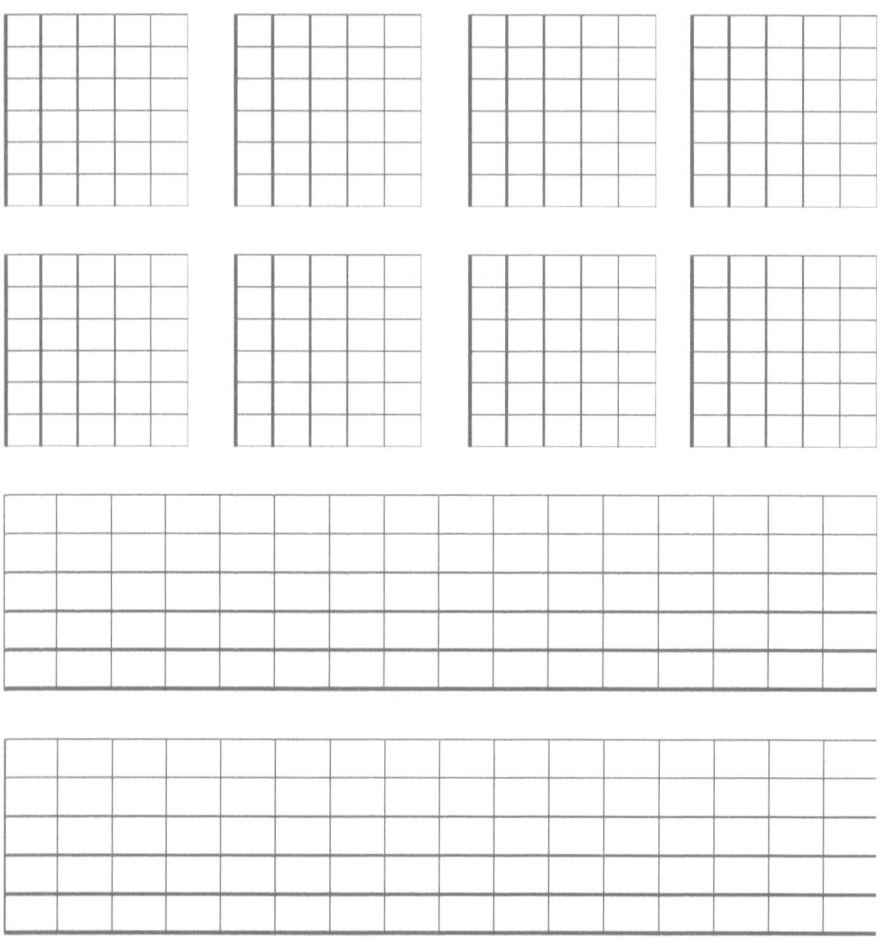

Notes

TAB

TAB

TAB

Date:

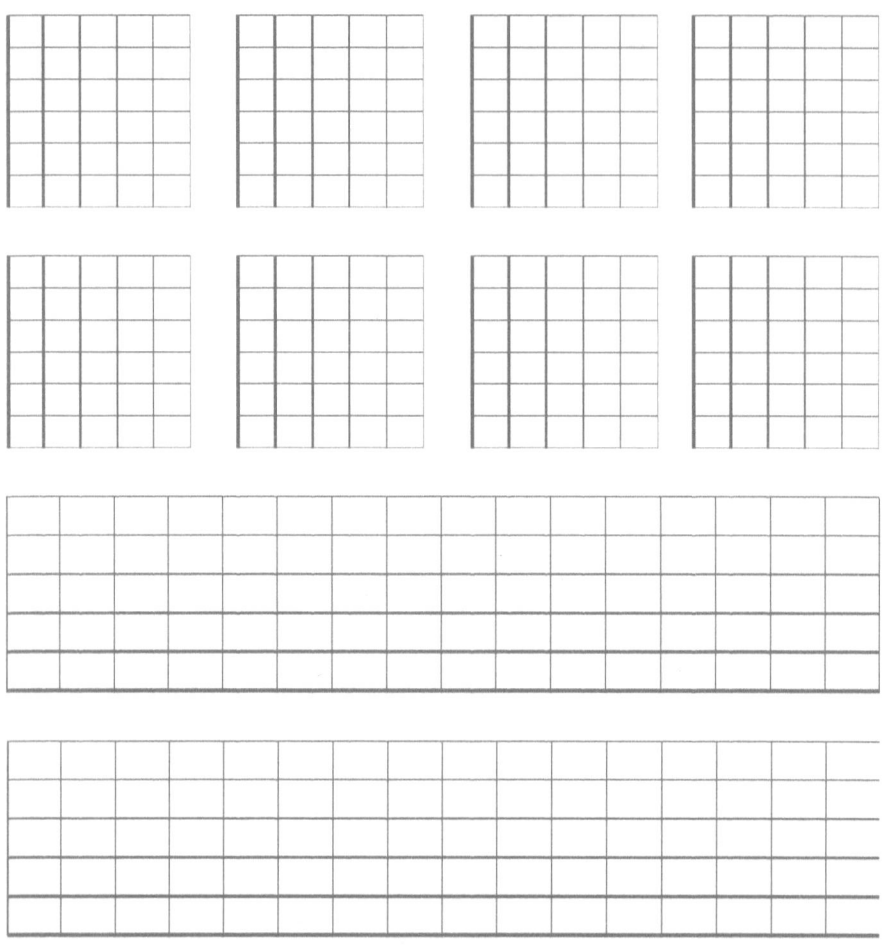

Notes

TAB

TAB

TAB

Date:

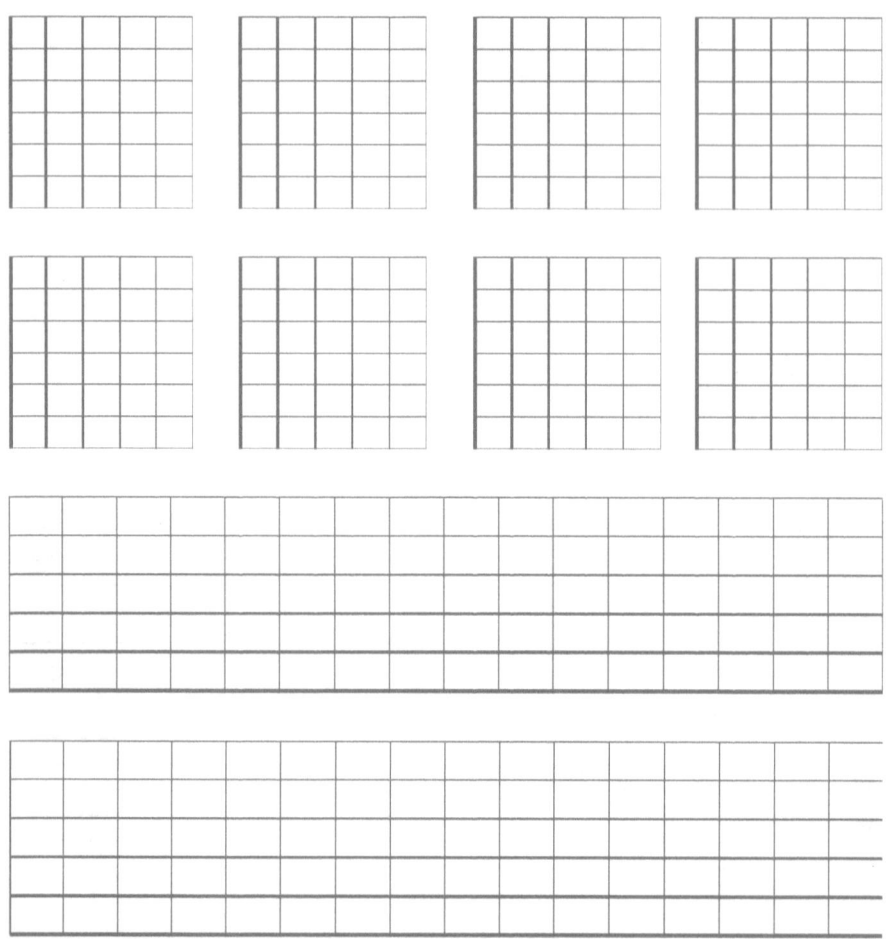

Notes

TAB

TAB

TAB

Date:

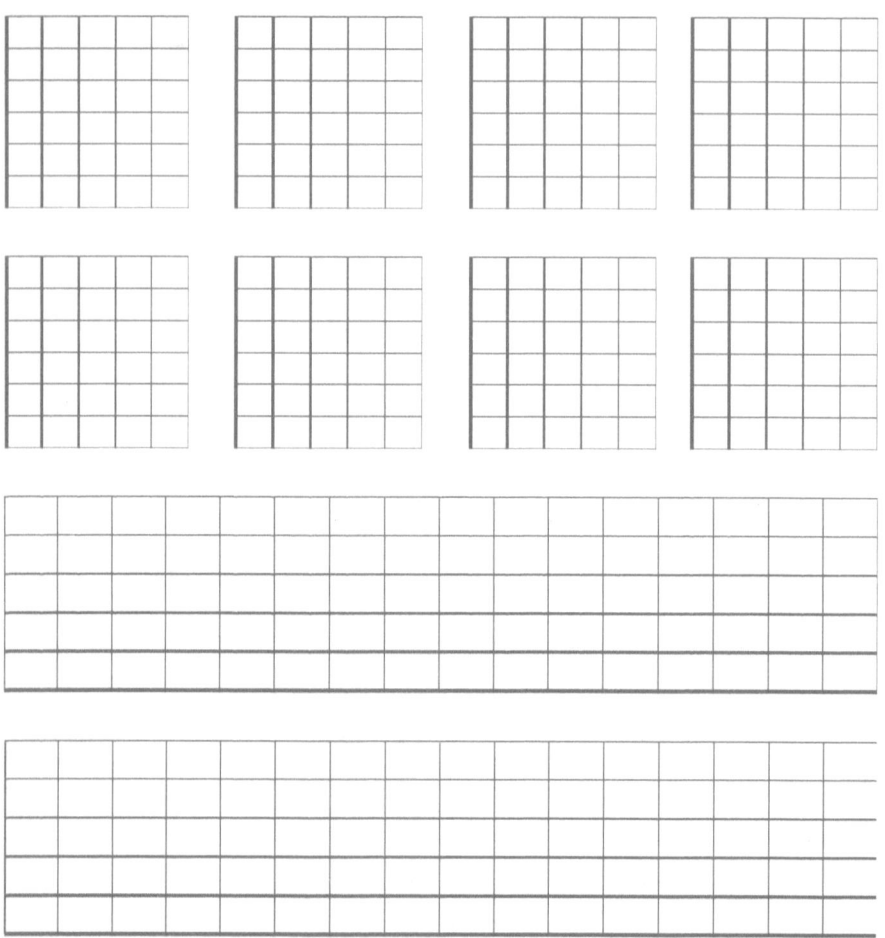

Notes

TAB

TAB

TAB

Date:

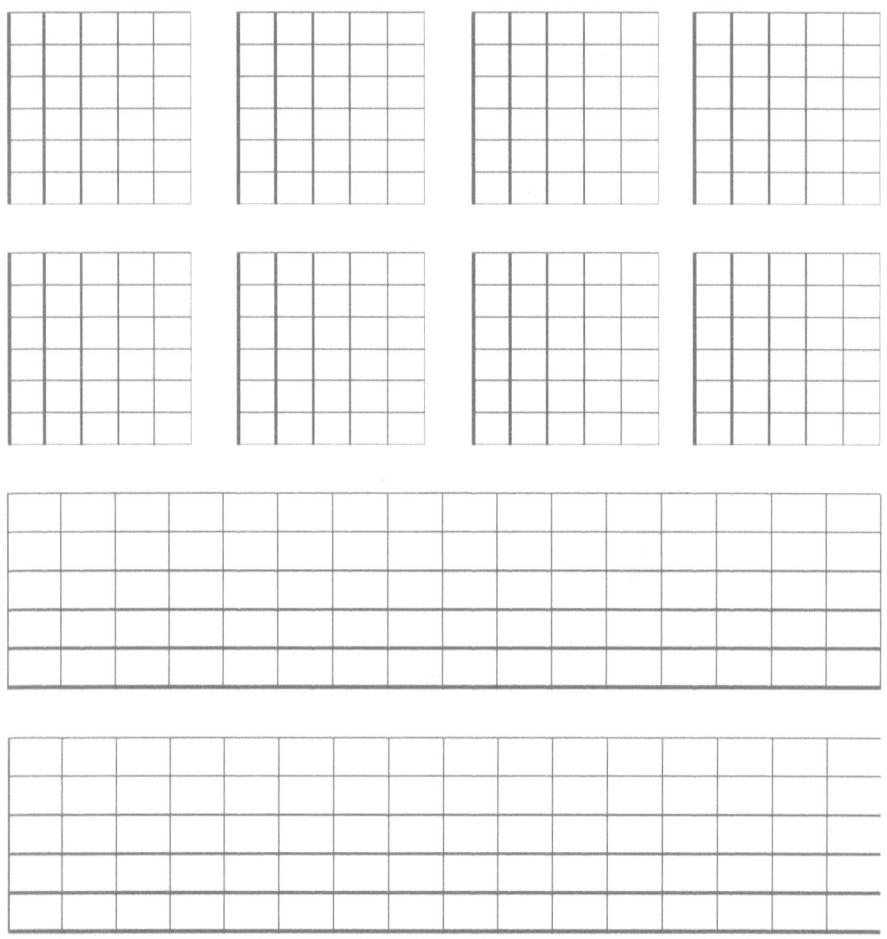

Notes

TAB

TAB

TAB

Date:

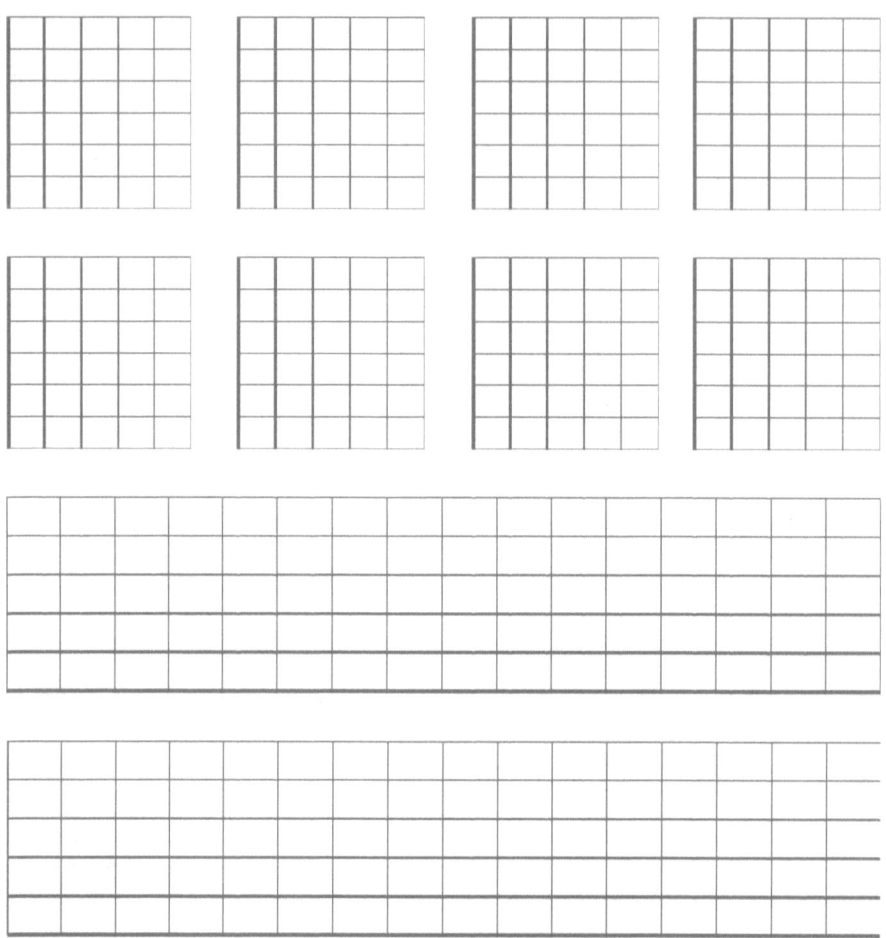

Notes

TAB

TAB

TAB

Date:

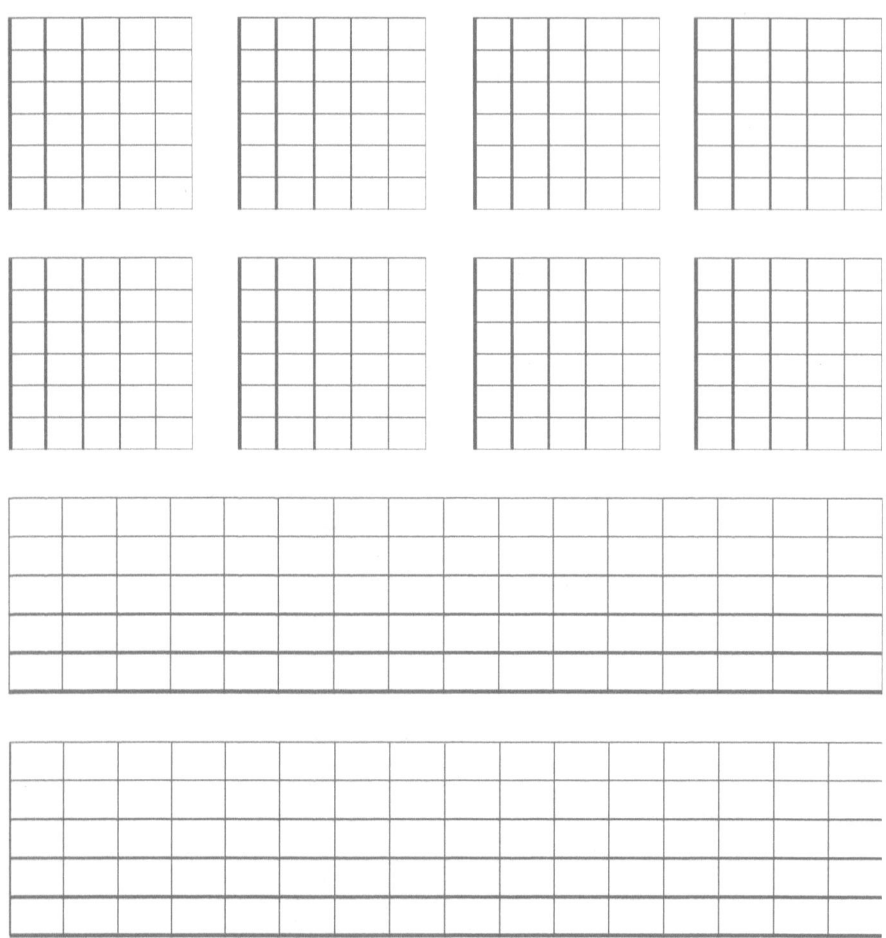

Notes

TAB

TAB

TAB

Date:

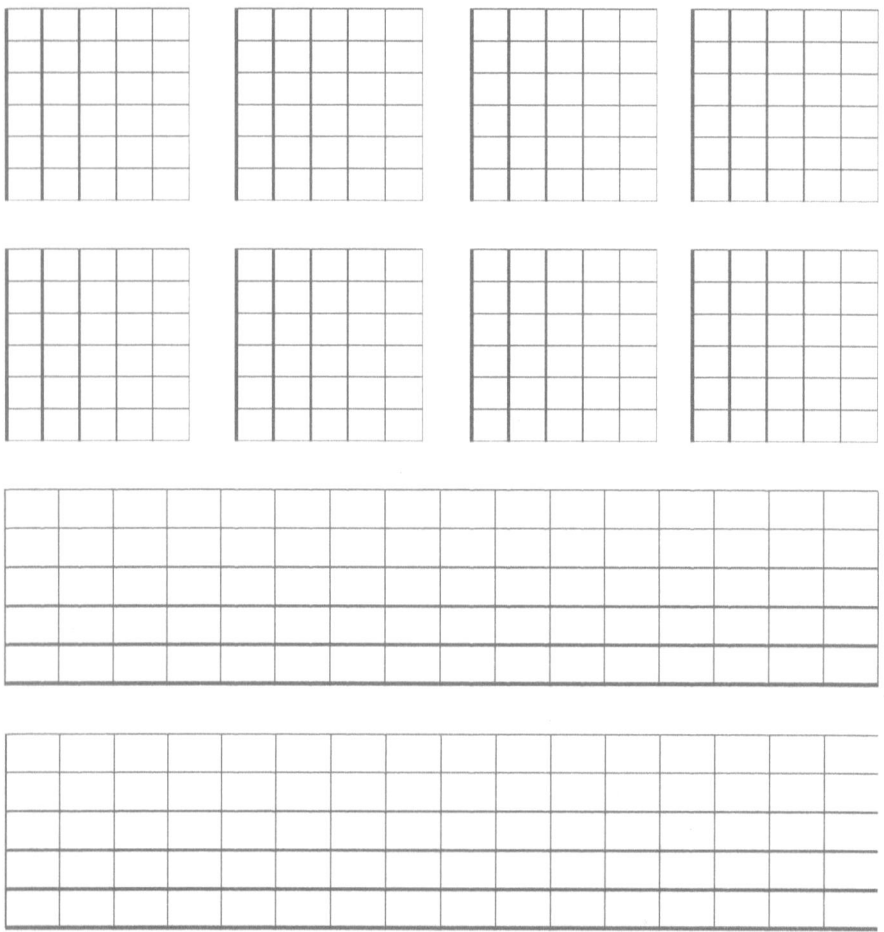

Notes

TAB

TAB

TAB

Date:

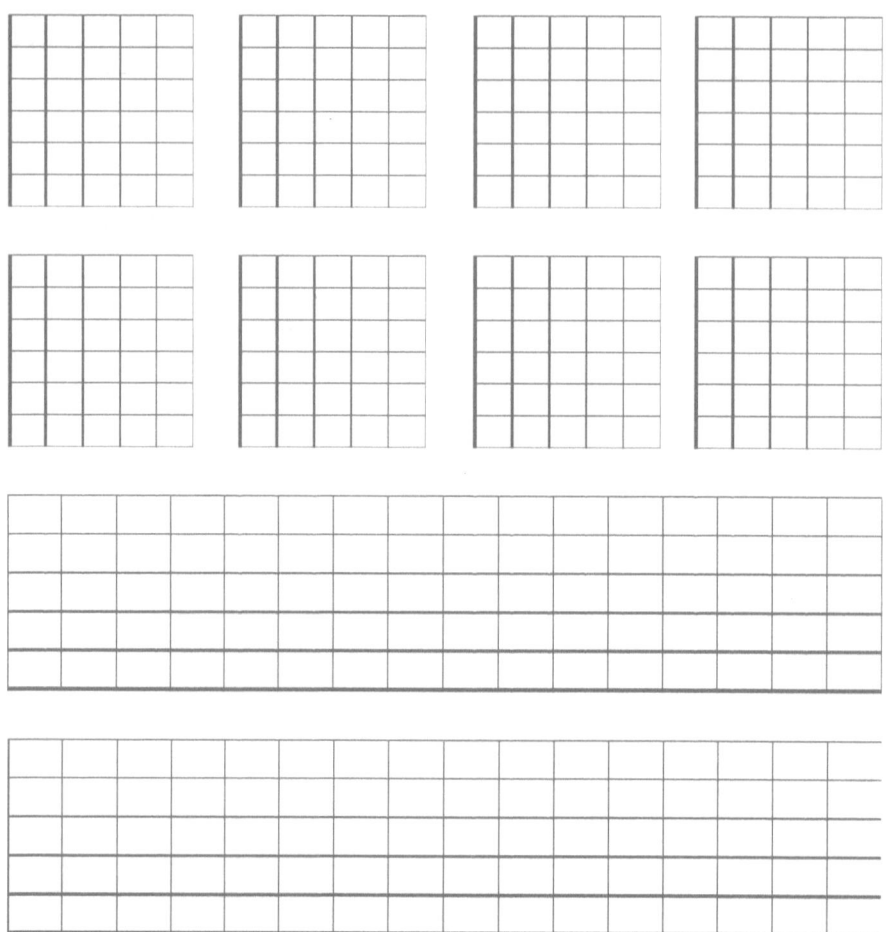

Notes

TAB

TAB

TAB

Date:

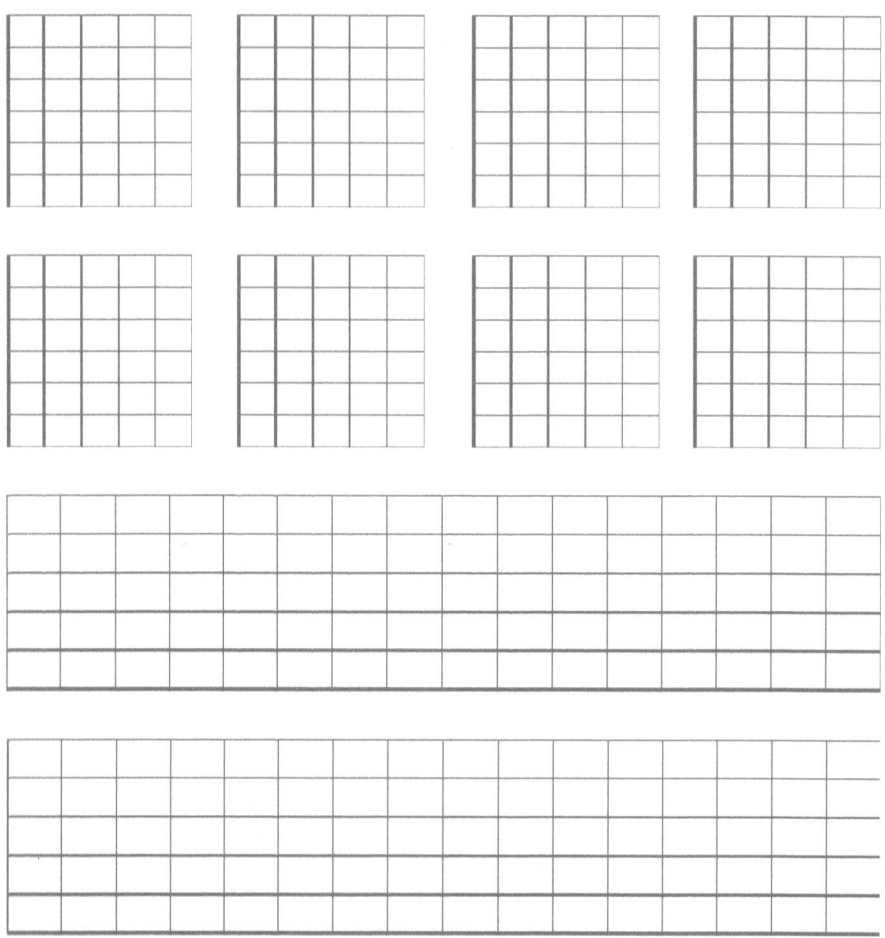

Notes

TAB

TAB

TAB

Date:

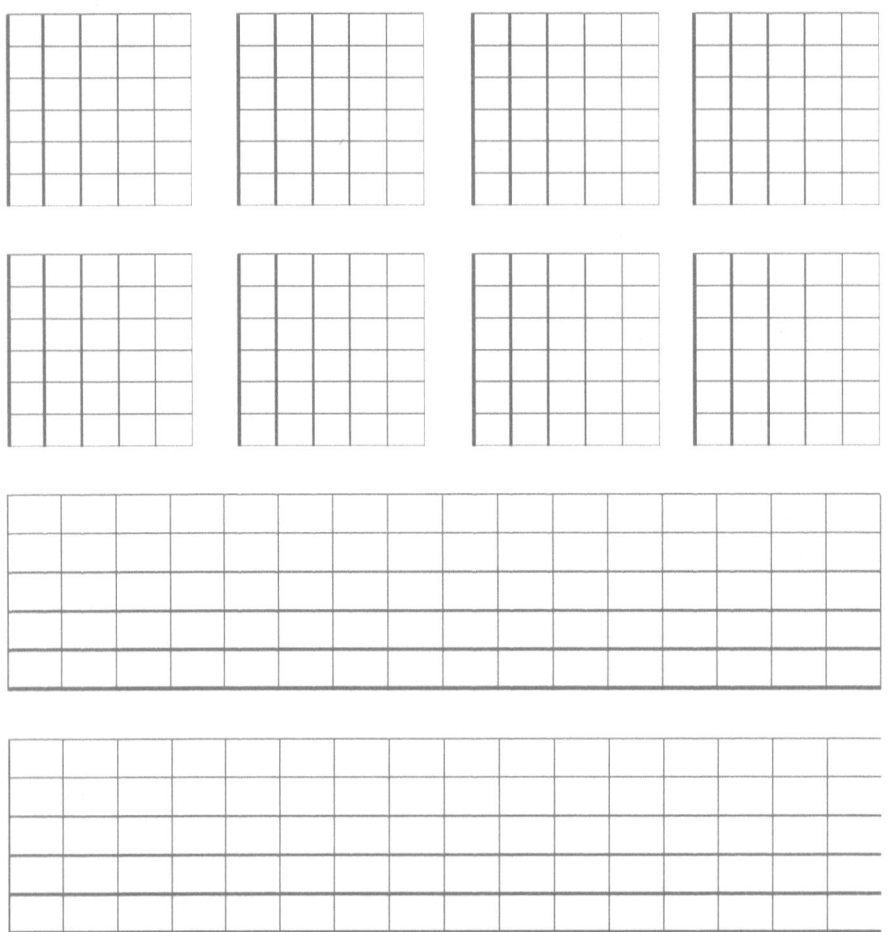

Notes

TAB

TAB

TAB

Date:

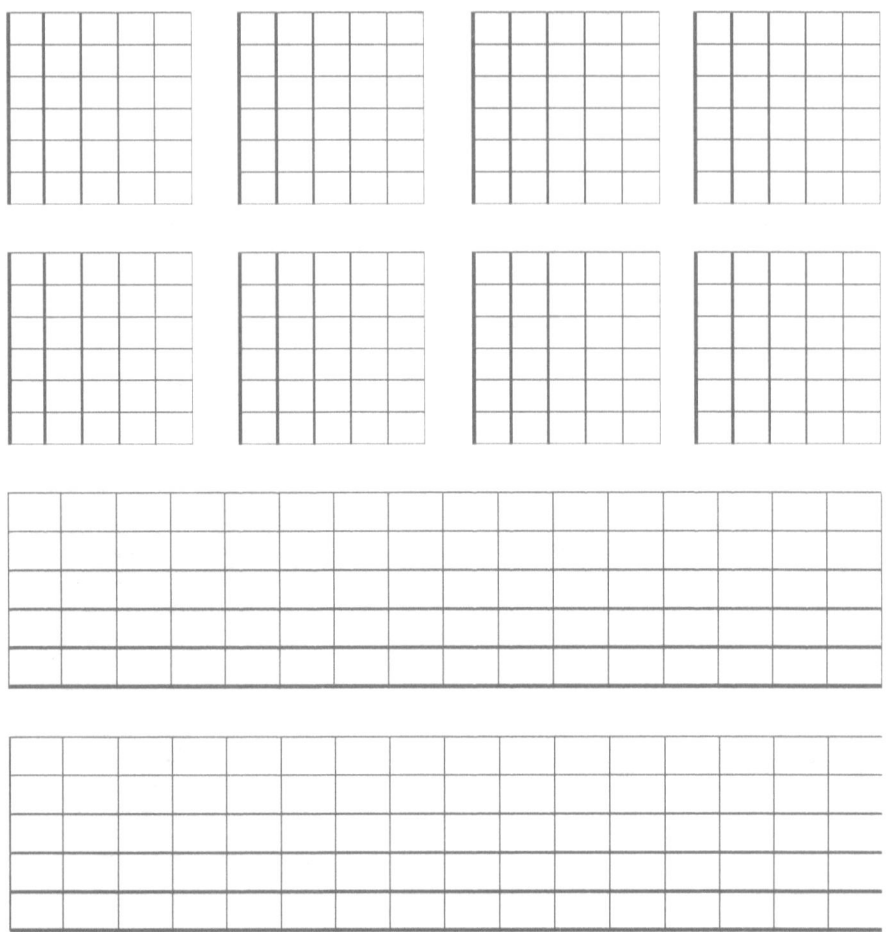

Notes

TAB

TAB

TAB

Date:

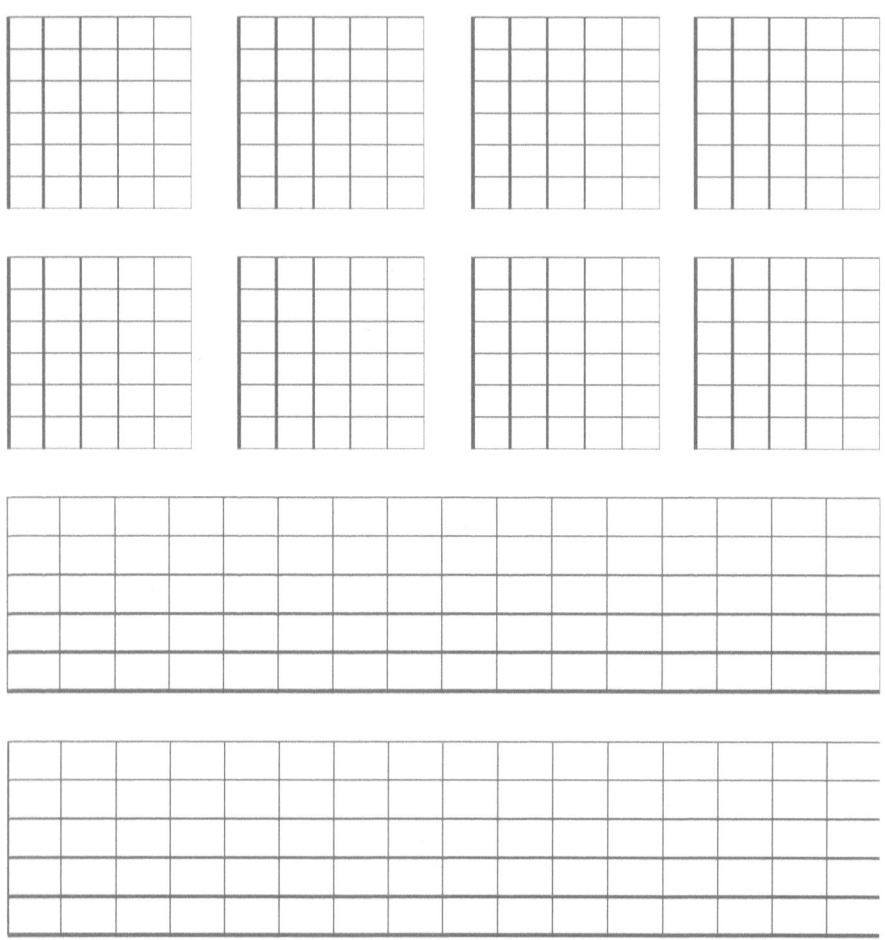

Notes

TAB

TAB

TAB

Date:

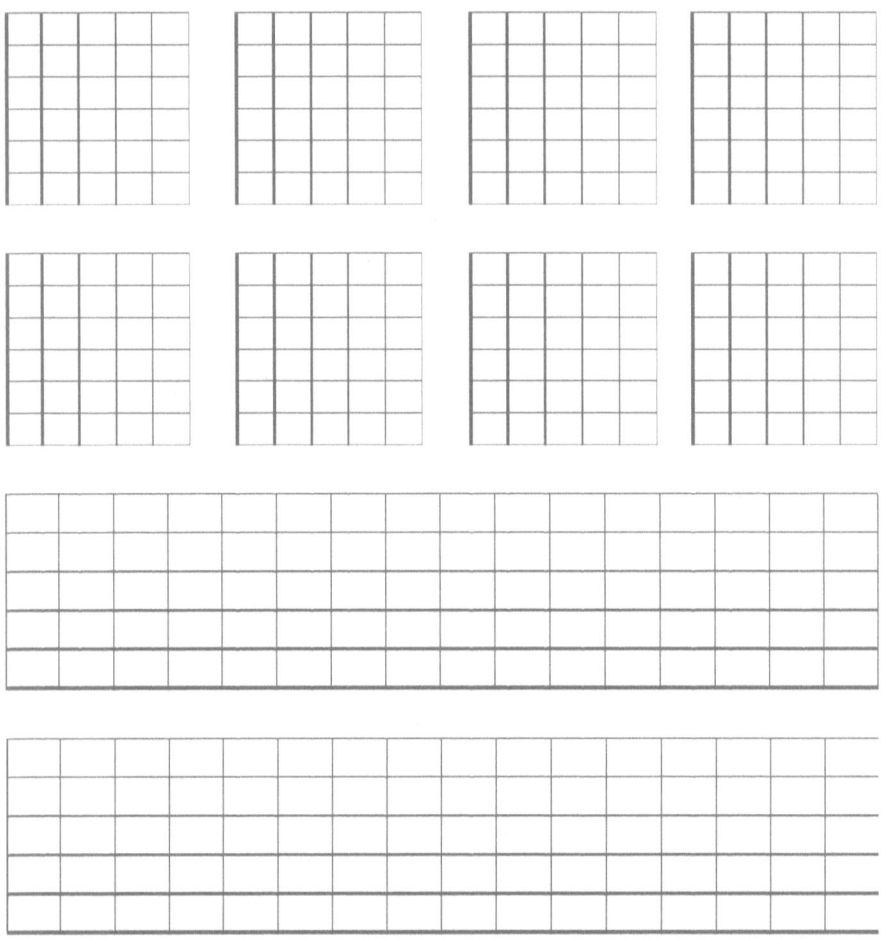

Notes

TAB

TAB

TAB

Date:

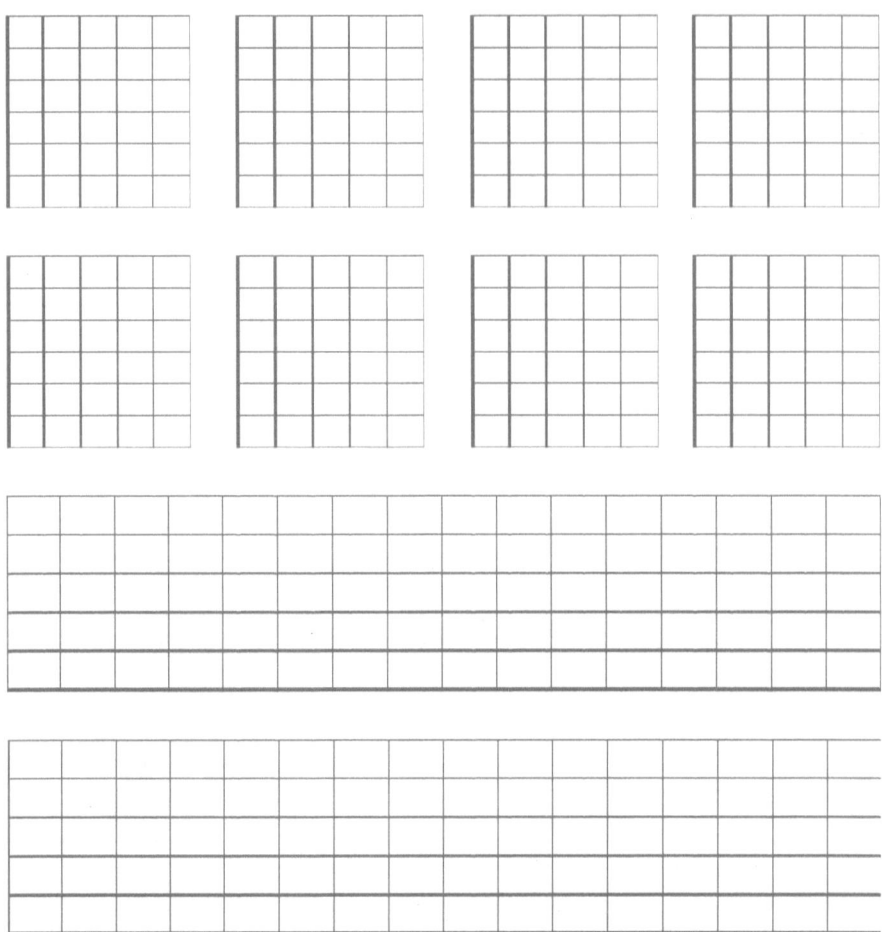

Notes

TAB

TAB

TAB

Date:

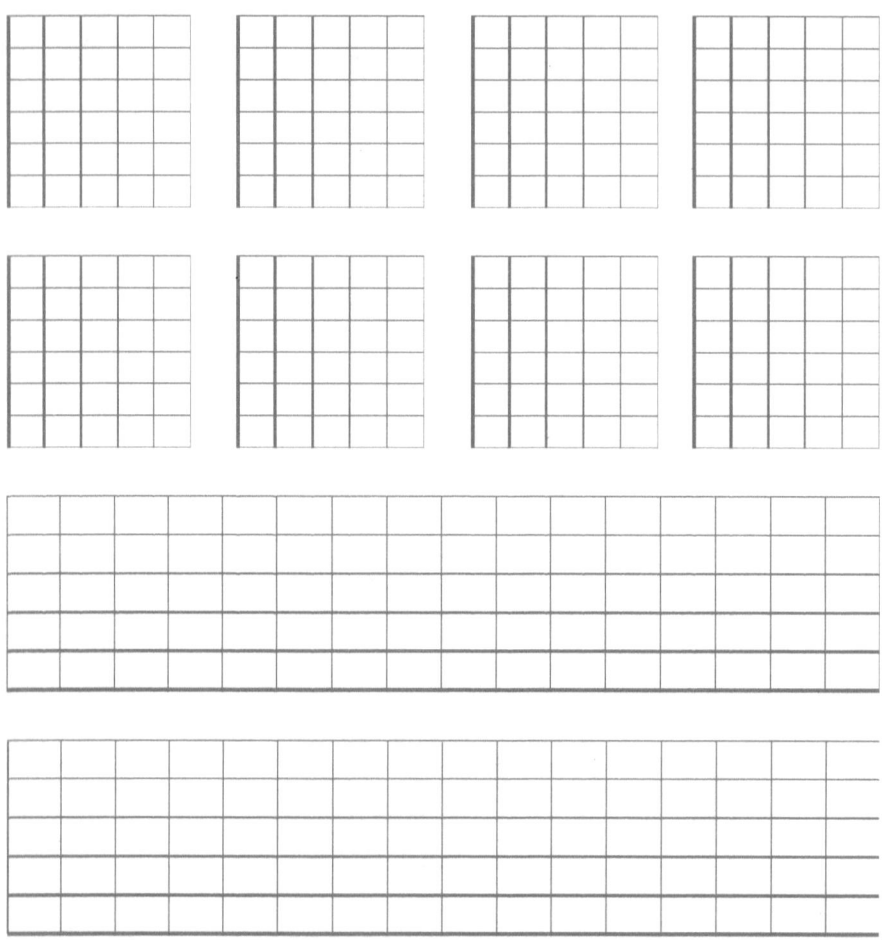

Notes

TAB

TAB

TAB

Date:

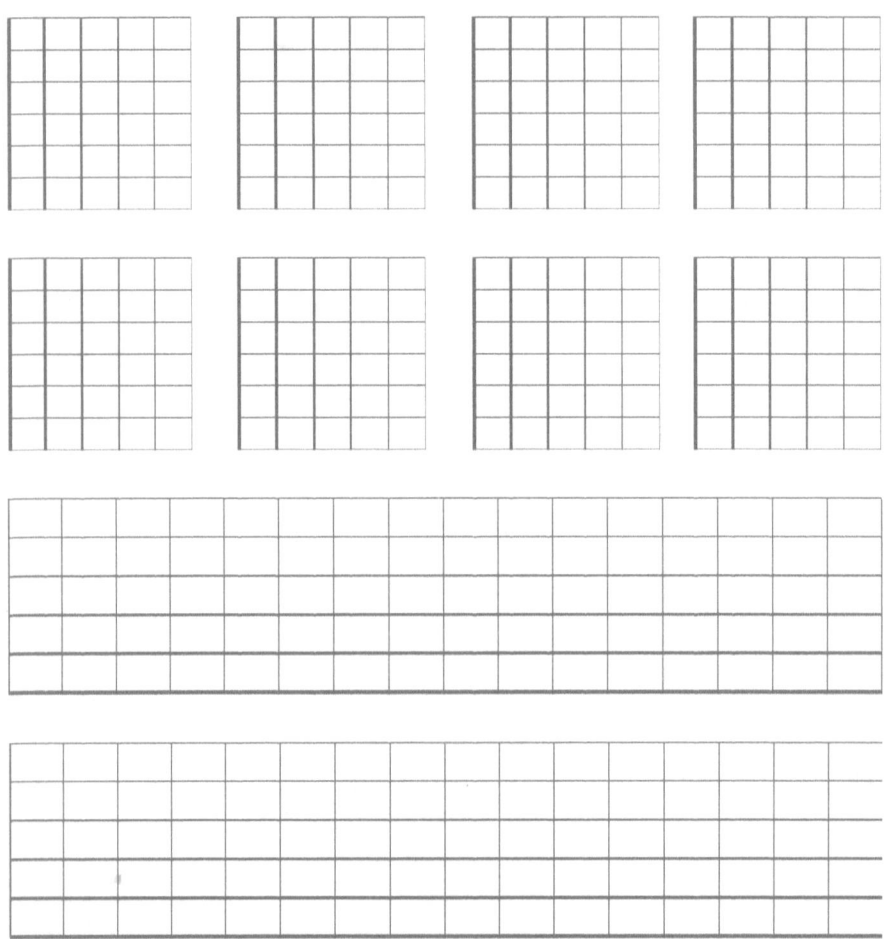

Notes

TAB

TAB

TAB

Date:

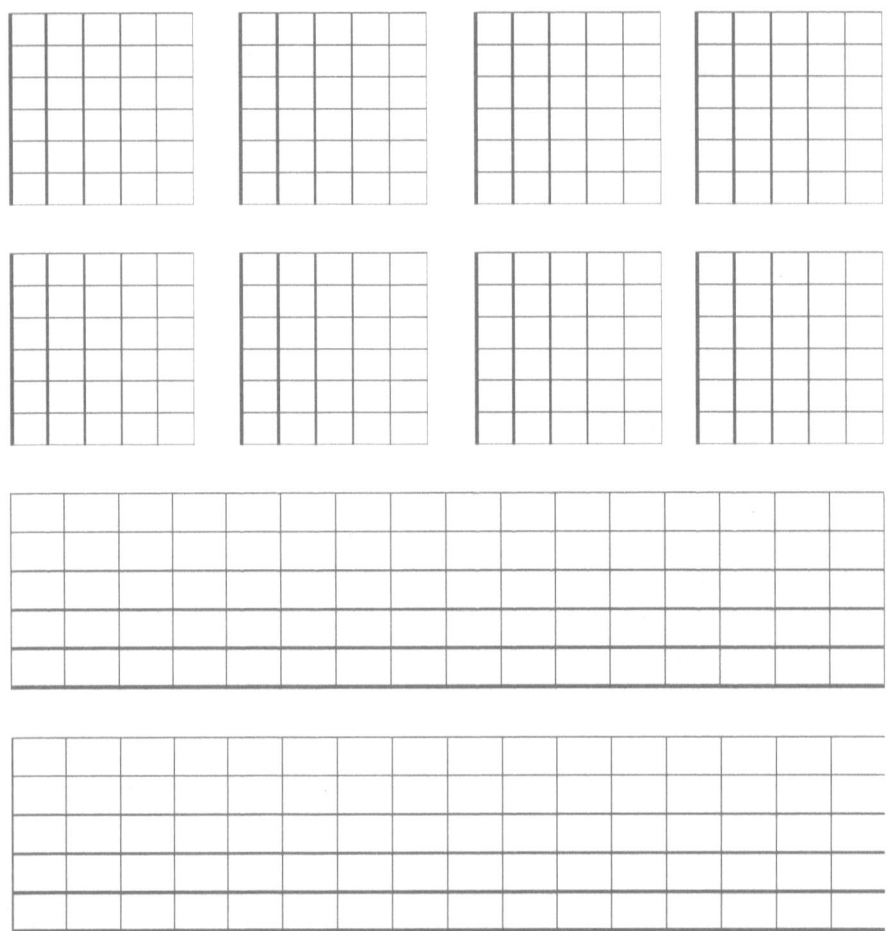

Notes

TAB

TAB

TAB

Date:

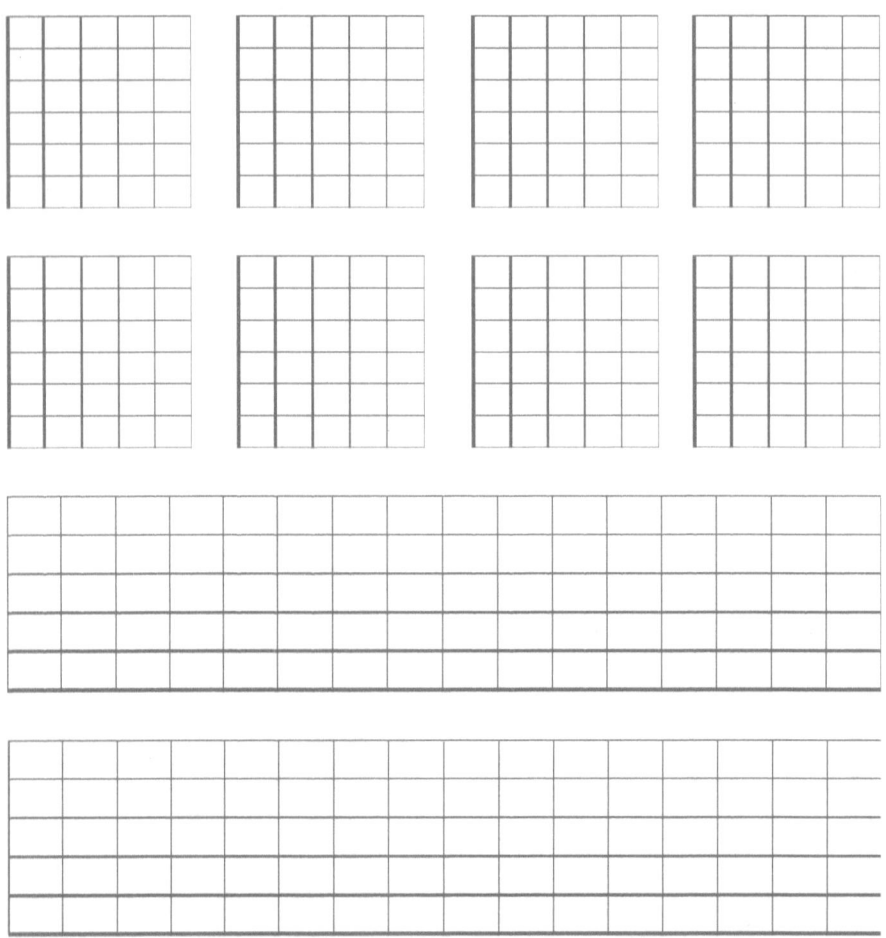

Notes

TAB

TAB

TAB

Date:

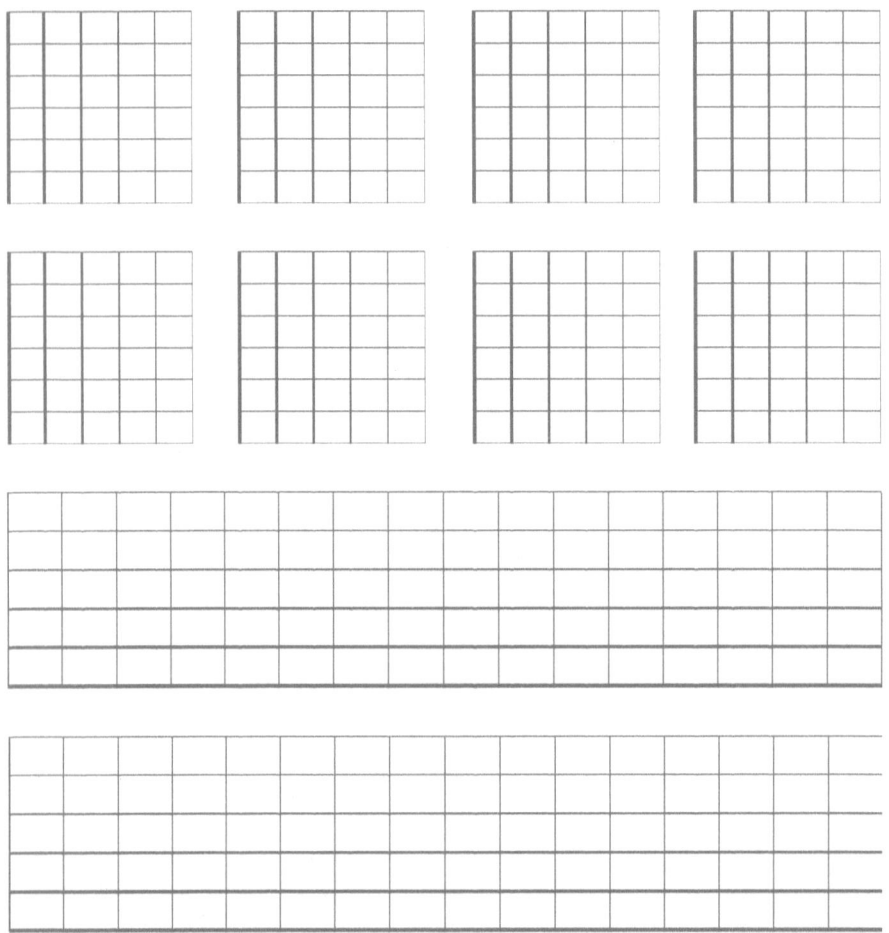

Notes

TAB

TAB

TAB

Date:

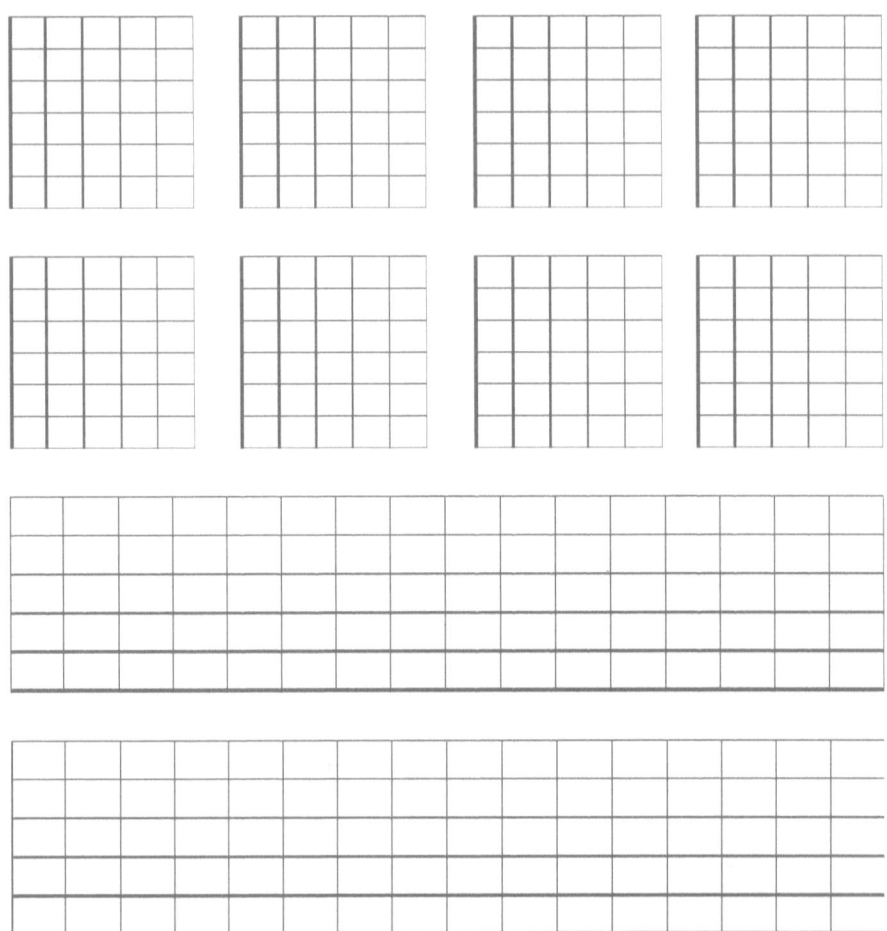

Notes

TAB

TAB

TAB

Date:

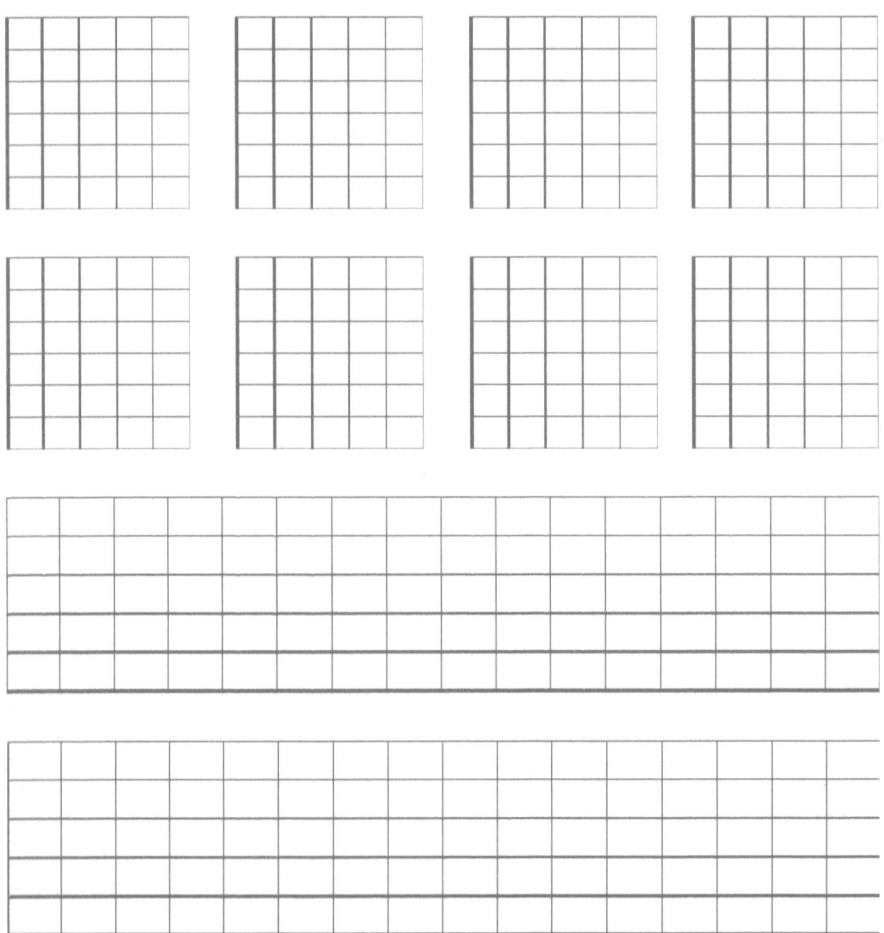

Notes

TAB

TAB

TAB

Date:

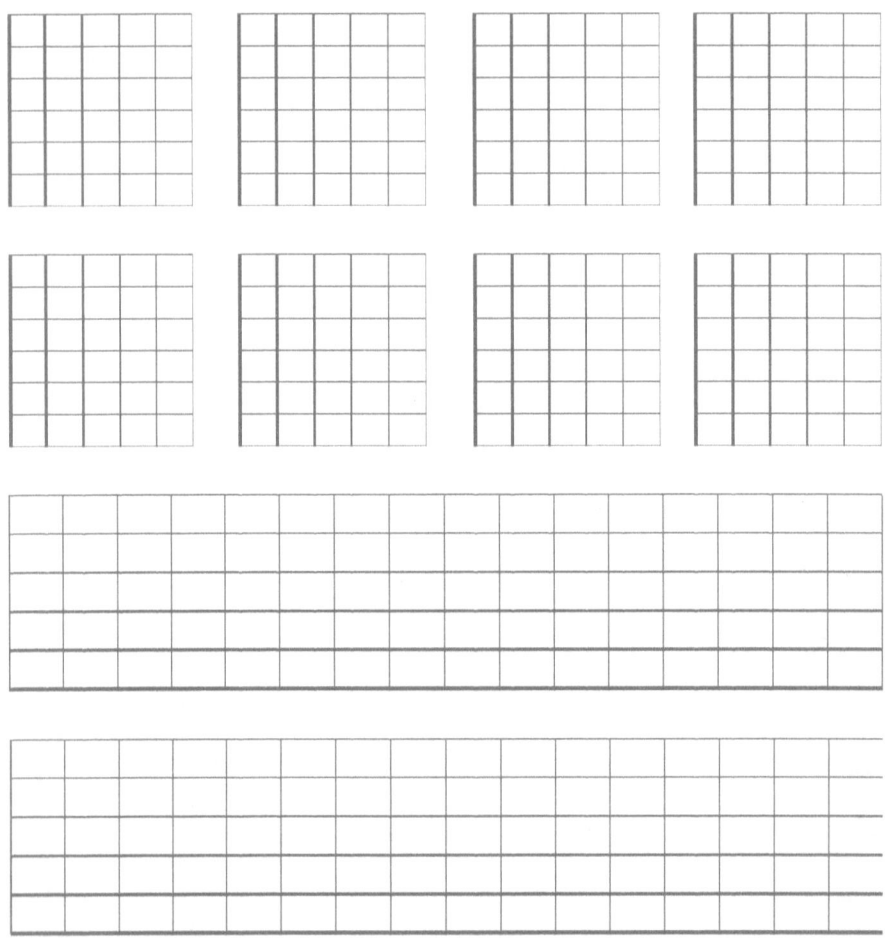

Notes

TAB

TAB

TAB

Date:

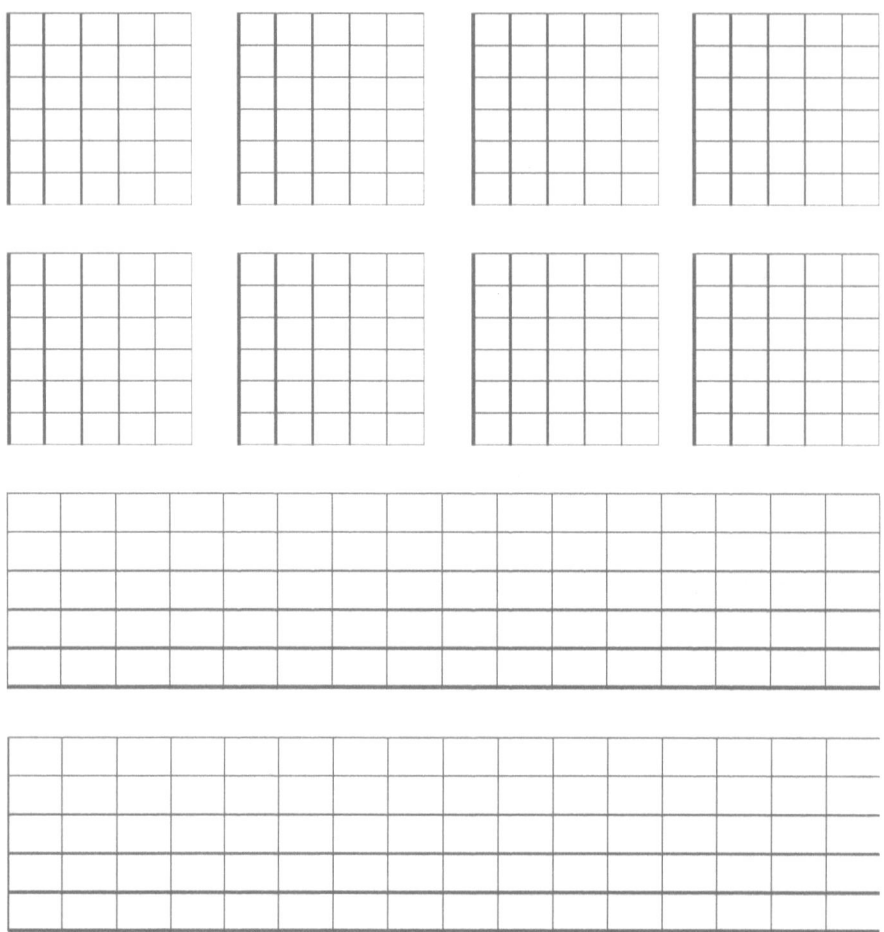

Notes

TAB

TAB

TAB

Date:

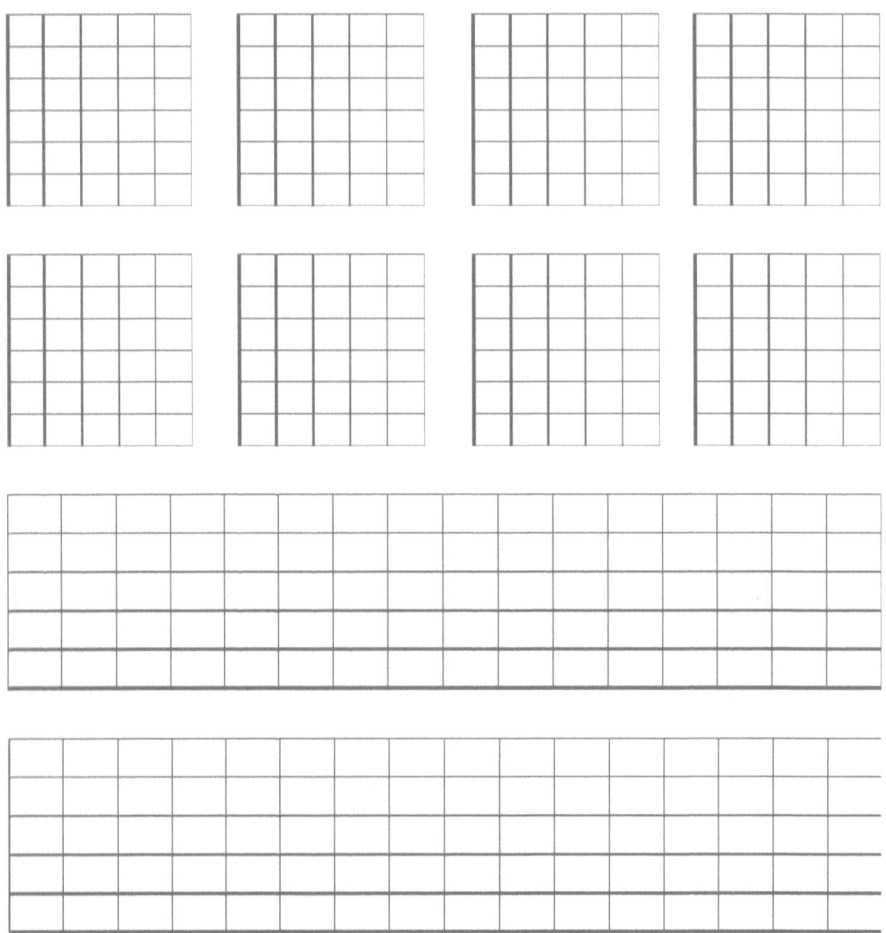

Notes

TAB

TAB

TAB

Date:

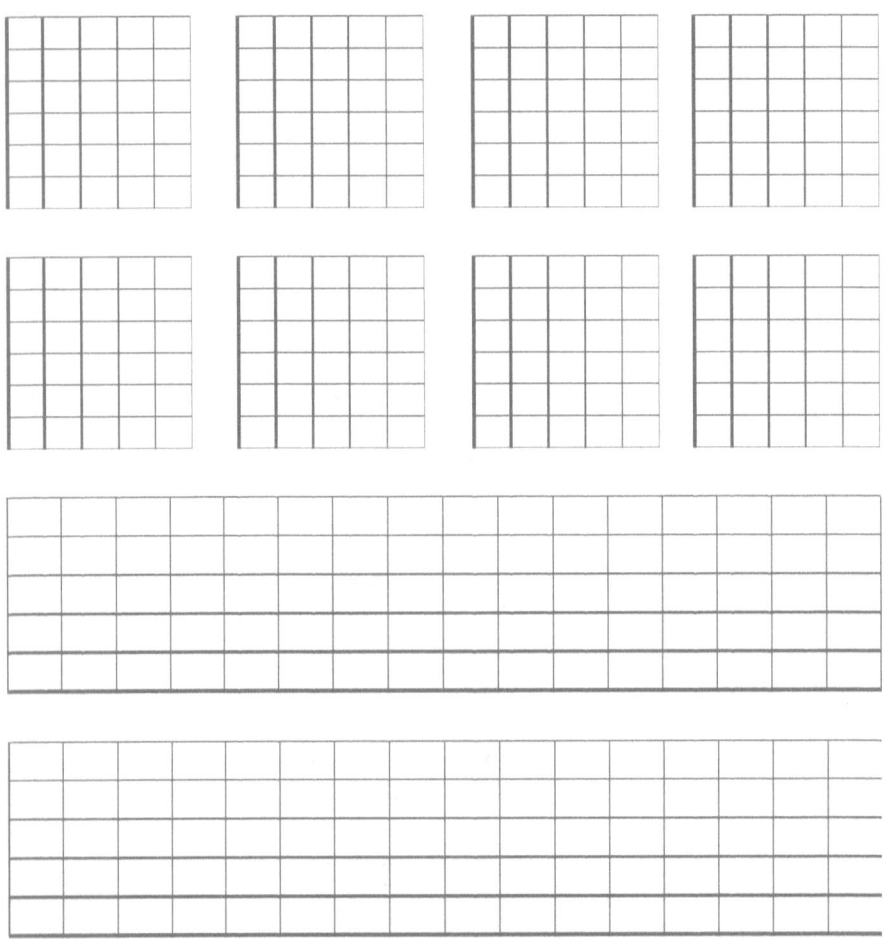

Notes

TAB

TAB

TAB

Date:

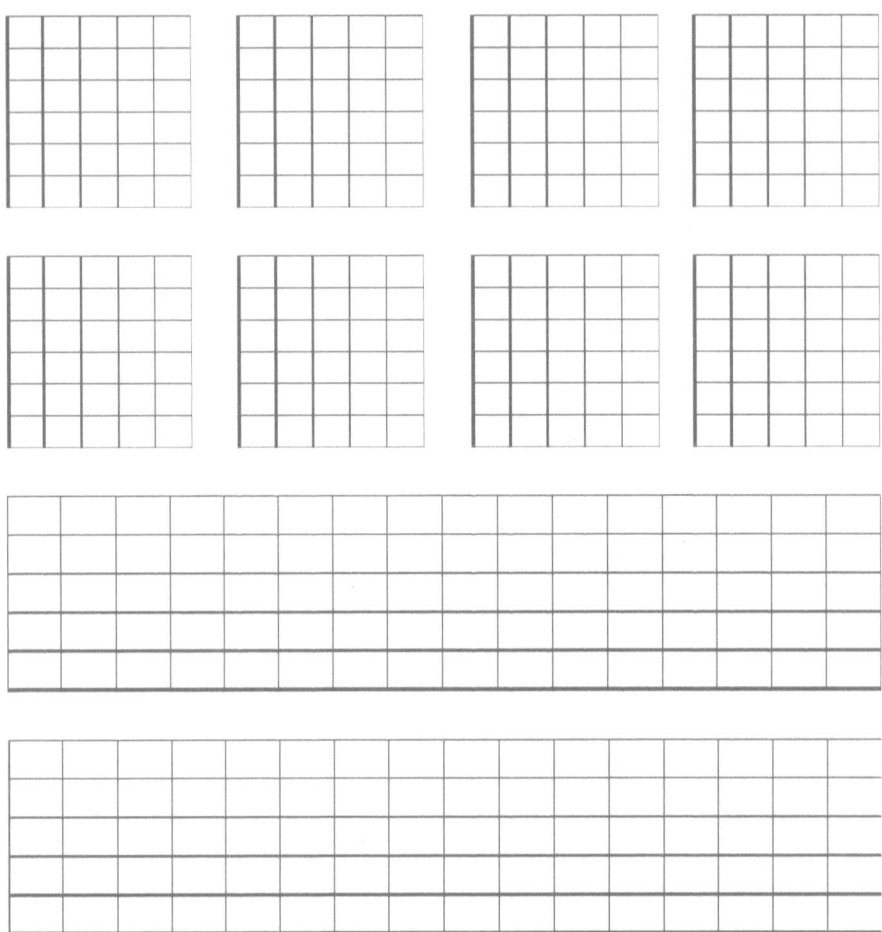

Notes

TAB

TAB

TAB

Date:

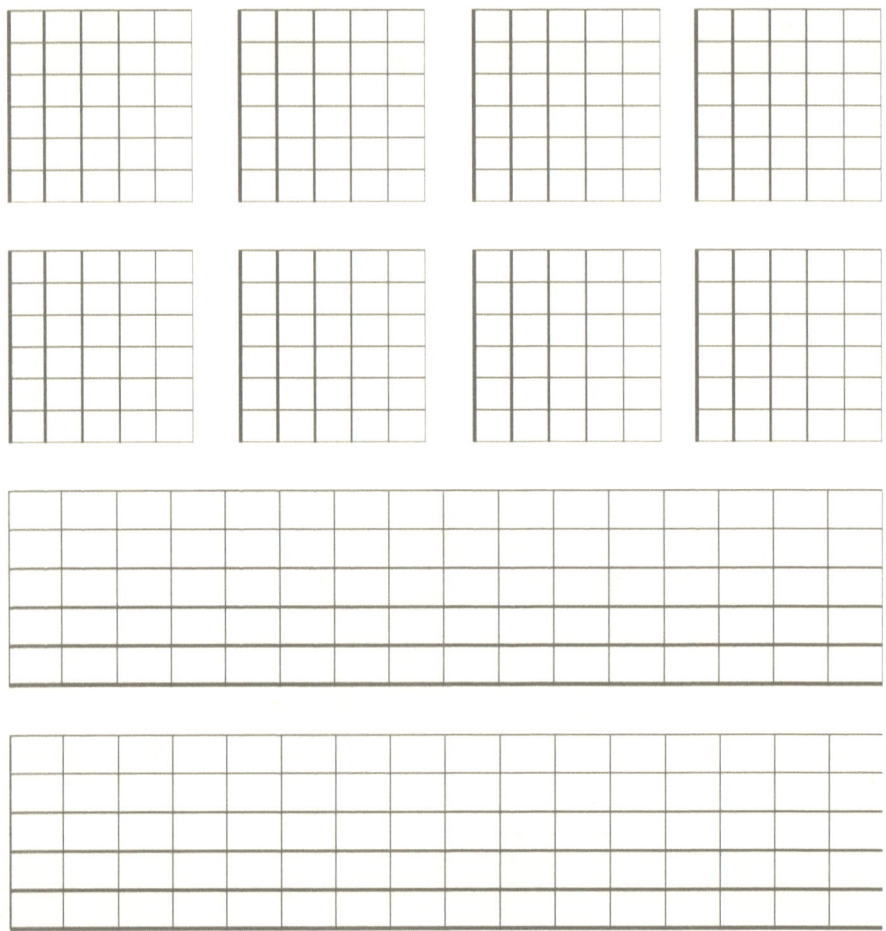

Notes

TAB

TAB

TAB

Date:

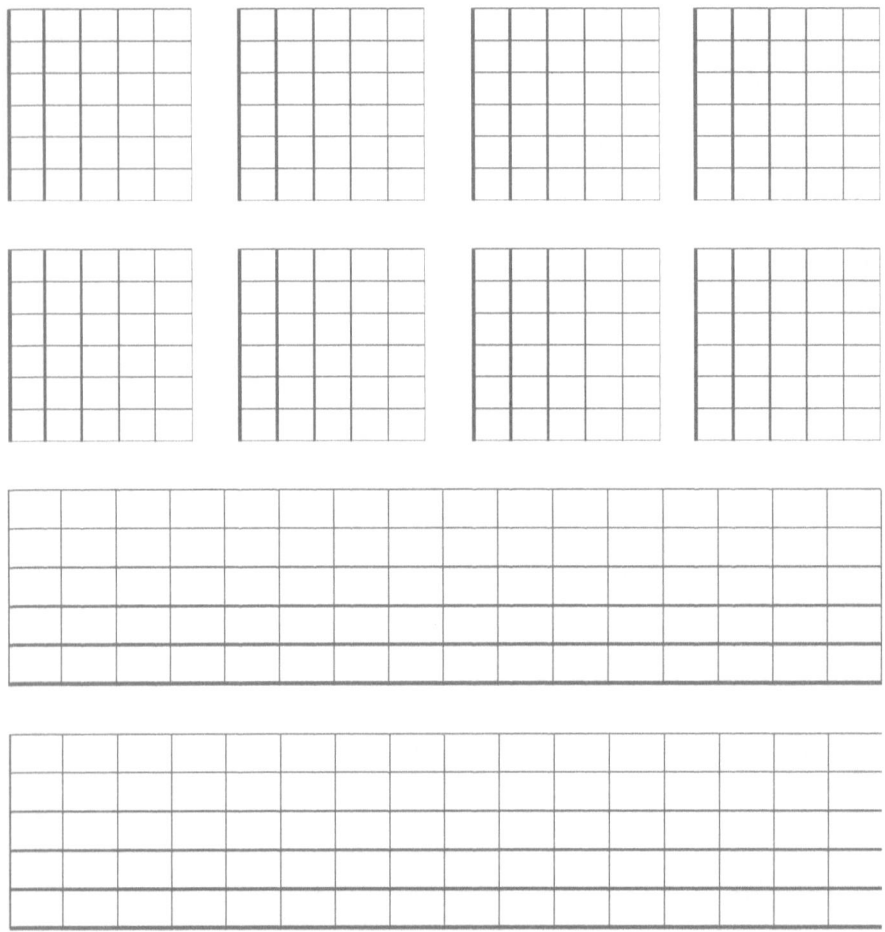

Notes

TAB

TAB

TAB

Date:

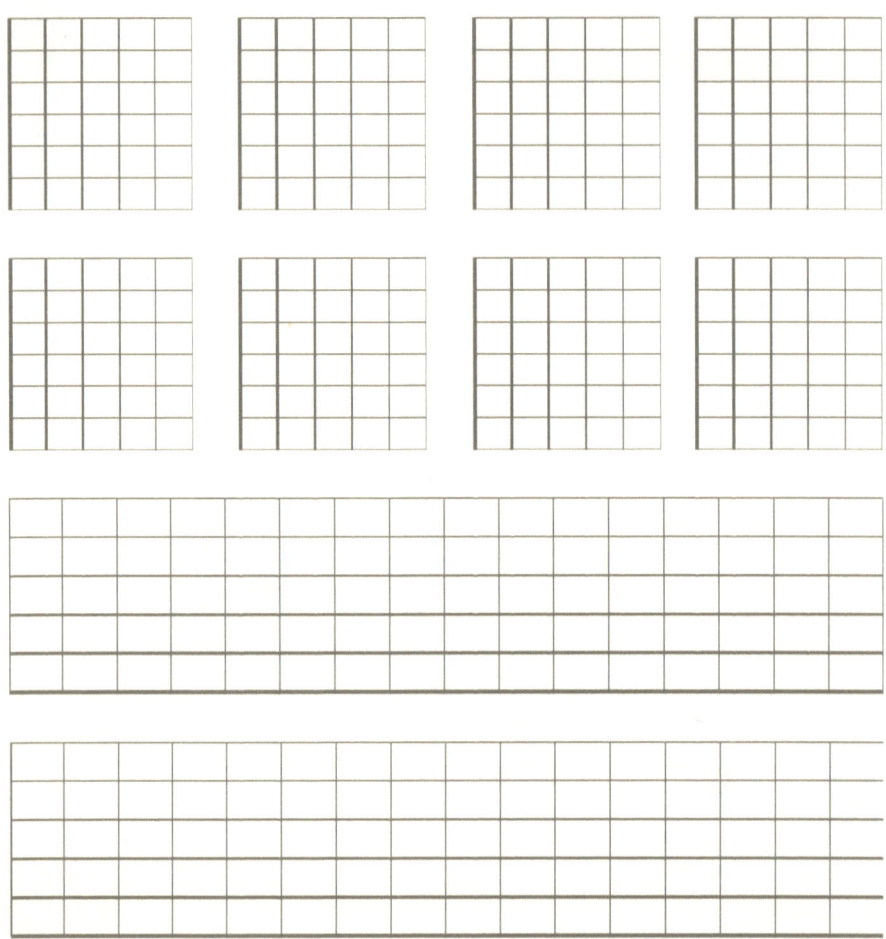

Notes

TAB

TAB

TAB

Date:

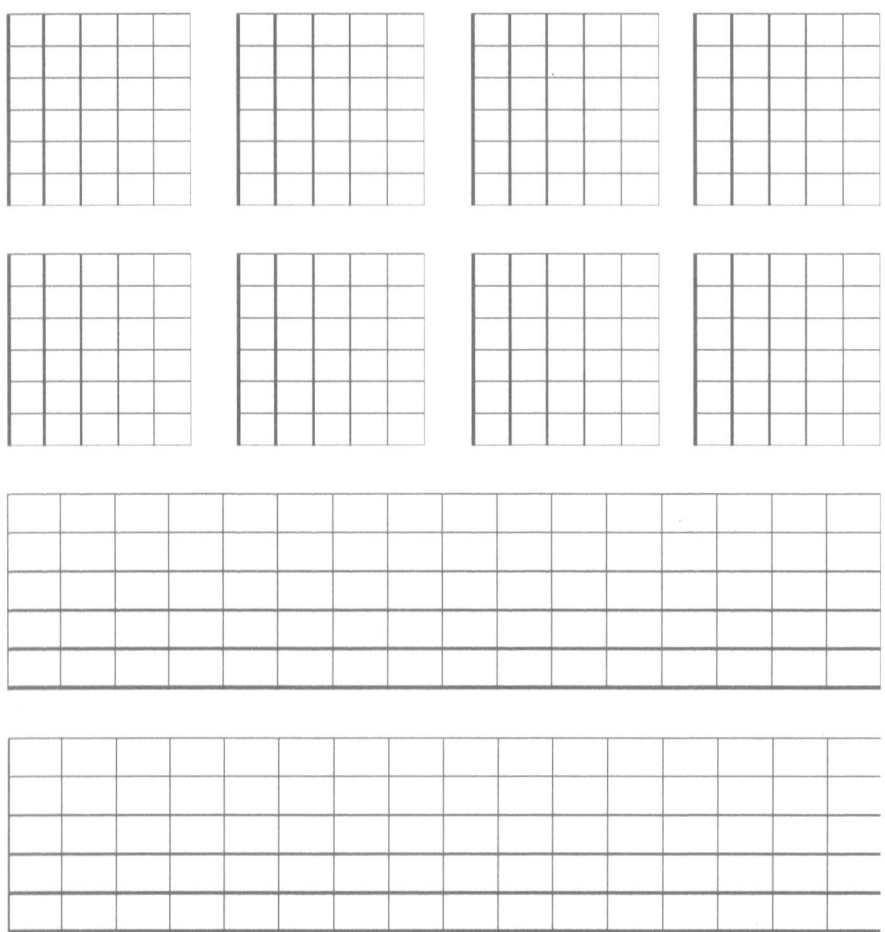

Notes

Date:

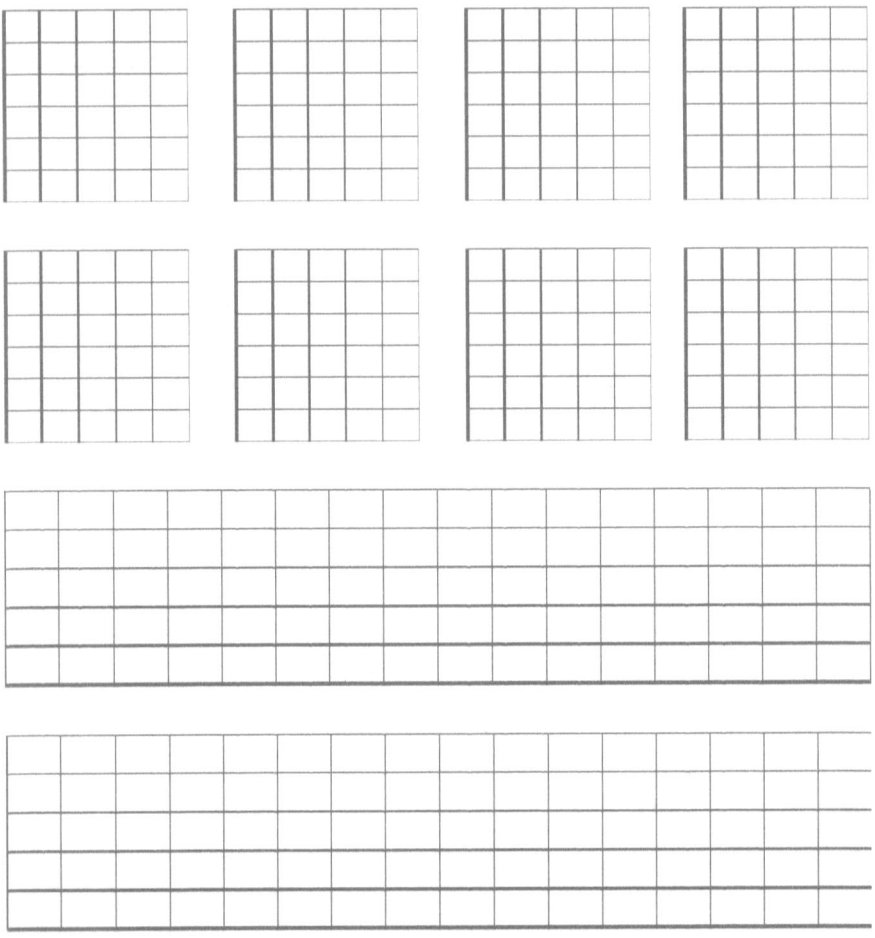

Notes

TAB

TAB

TAB

Date:

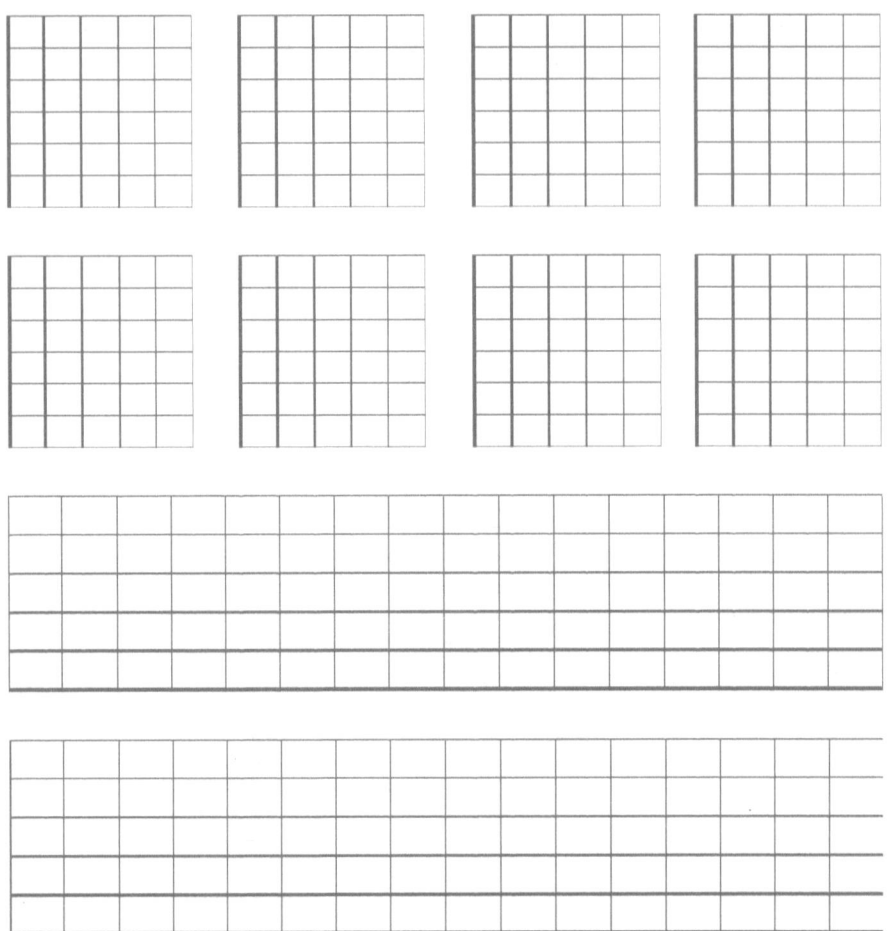

Notes

TAB

TAB

TAB

Date:

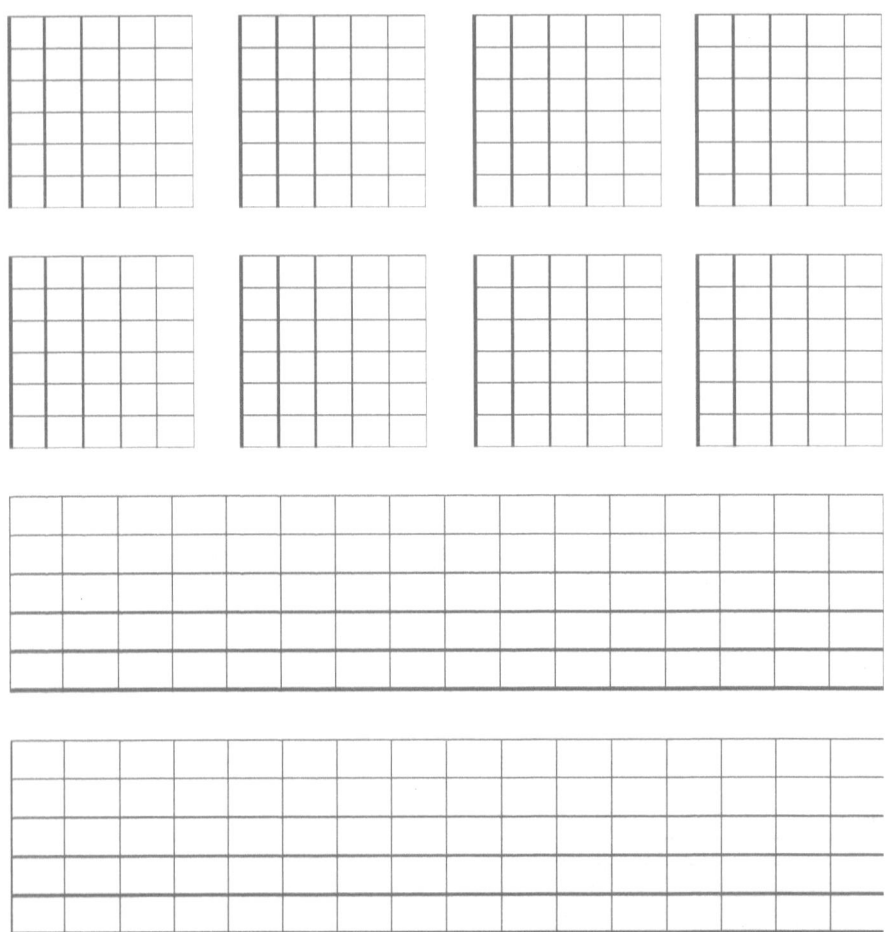

Notes

TAB

TAB

TAB

Date:

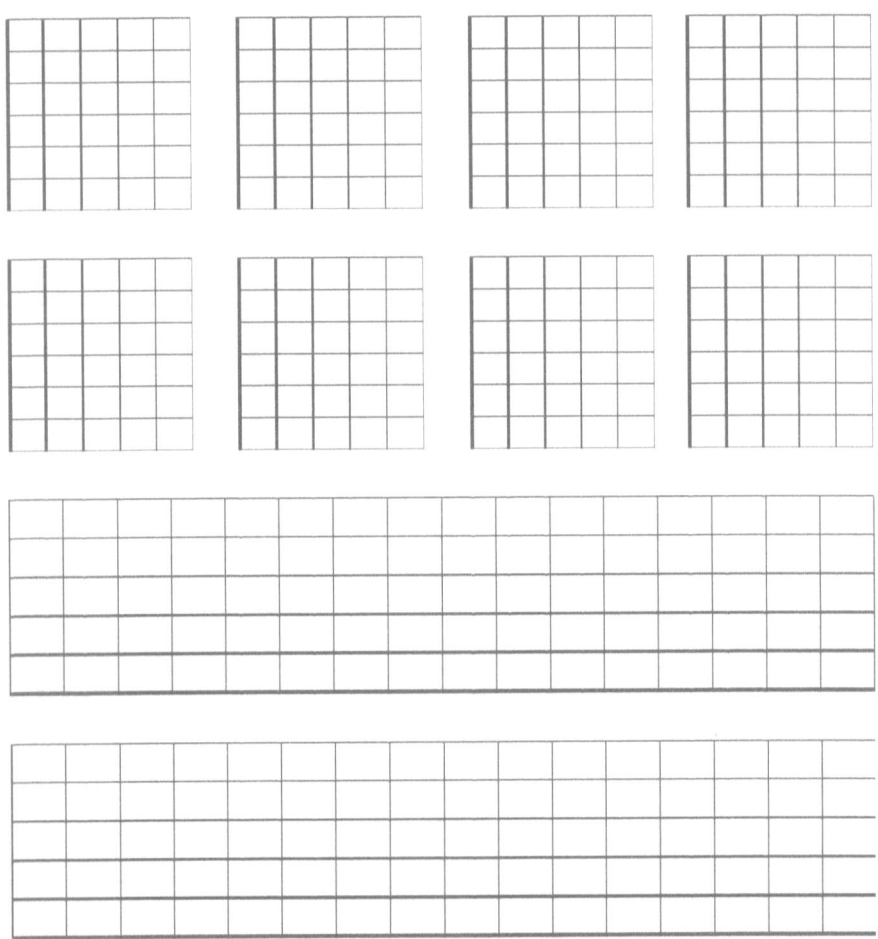

Notes

TAB

TAB

TAB

Date:

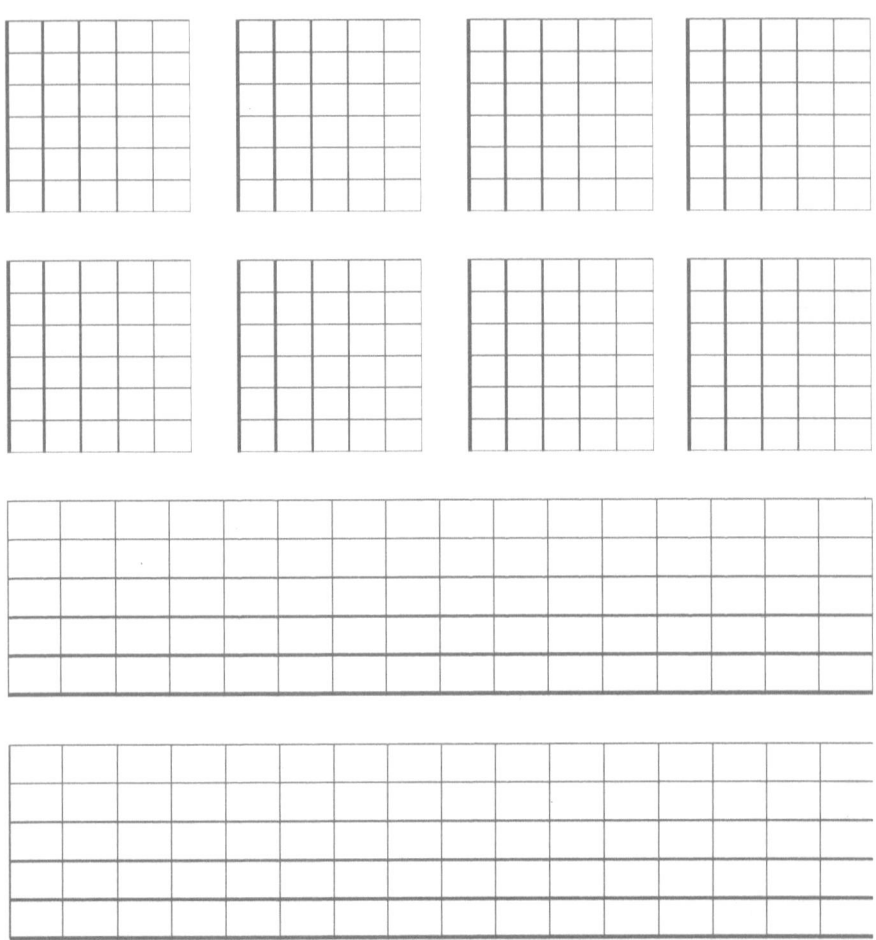

Notes

TAB

TAB

TAB

Date:

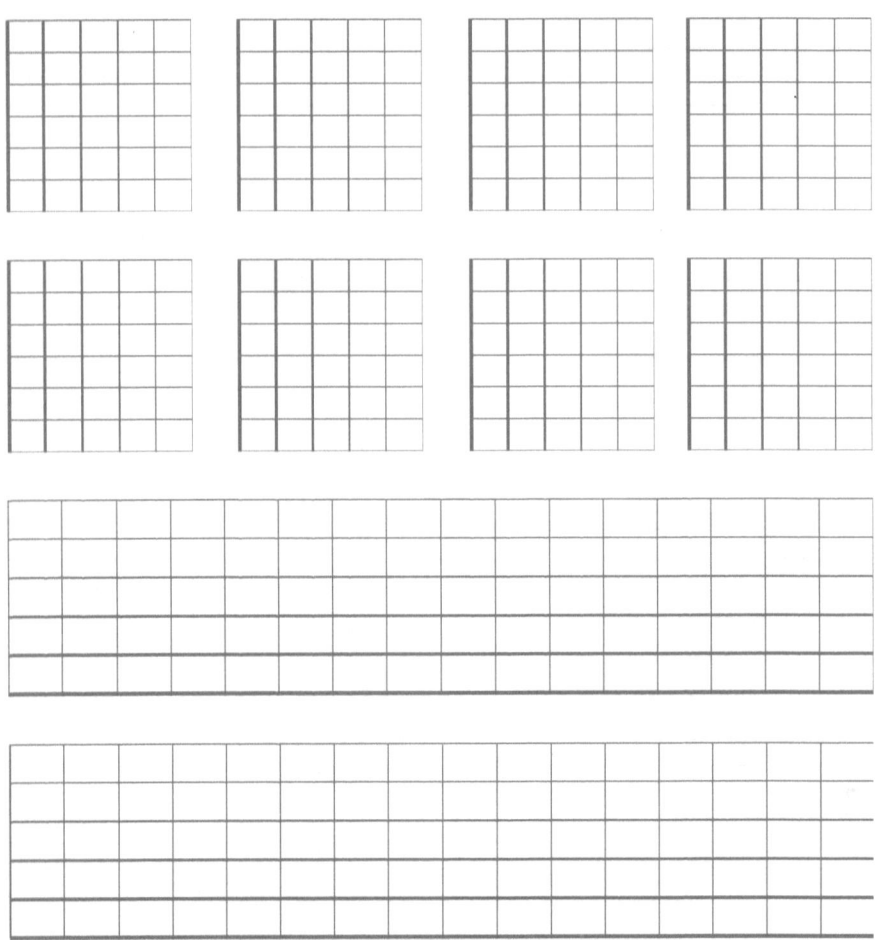

Notes

TAB

TAB

TAB

Date:

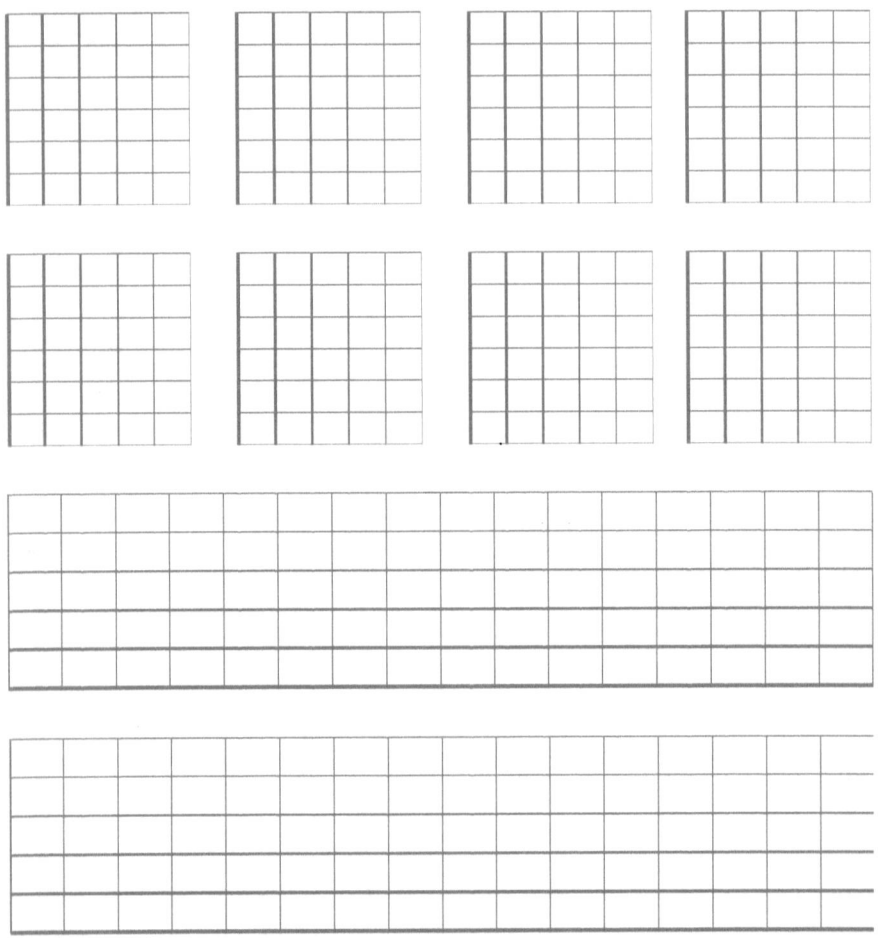

Notes

TAB

TAB

TAB

Date:

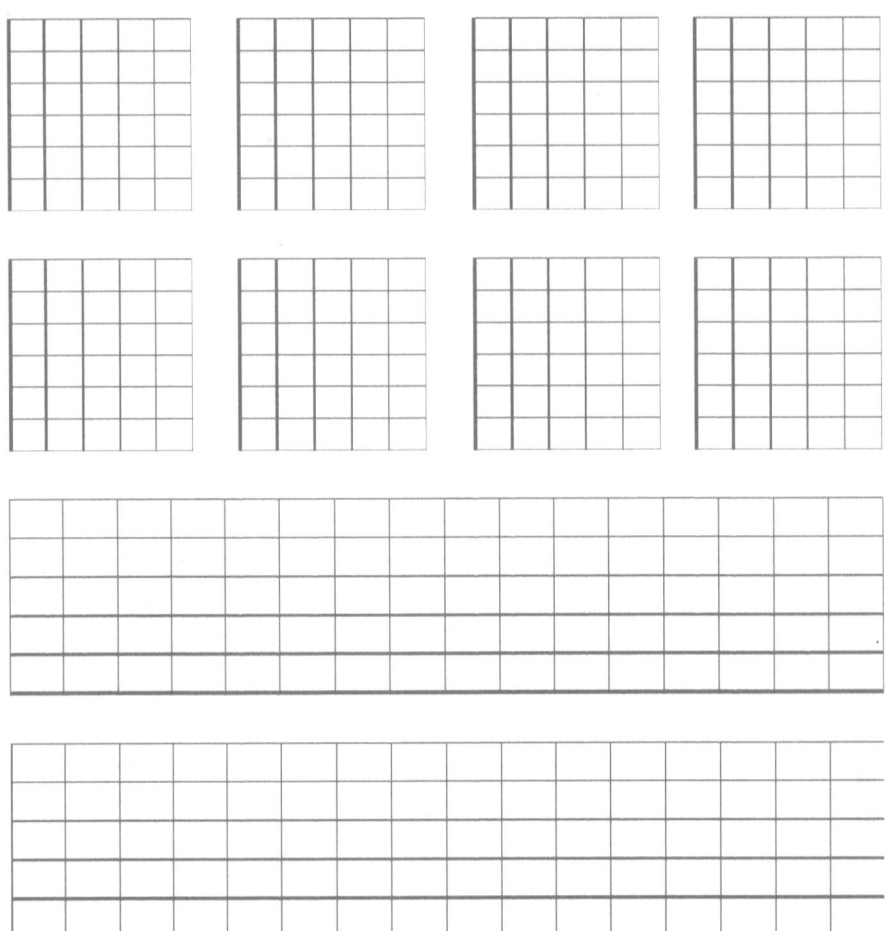

Notes

TAB

TAB

TAB

Date:

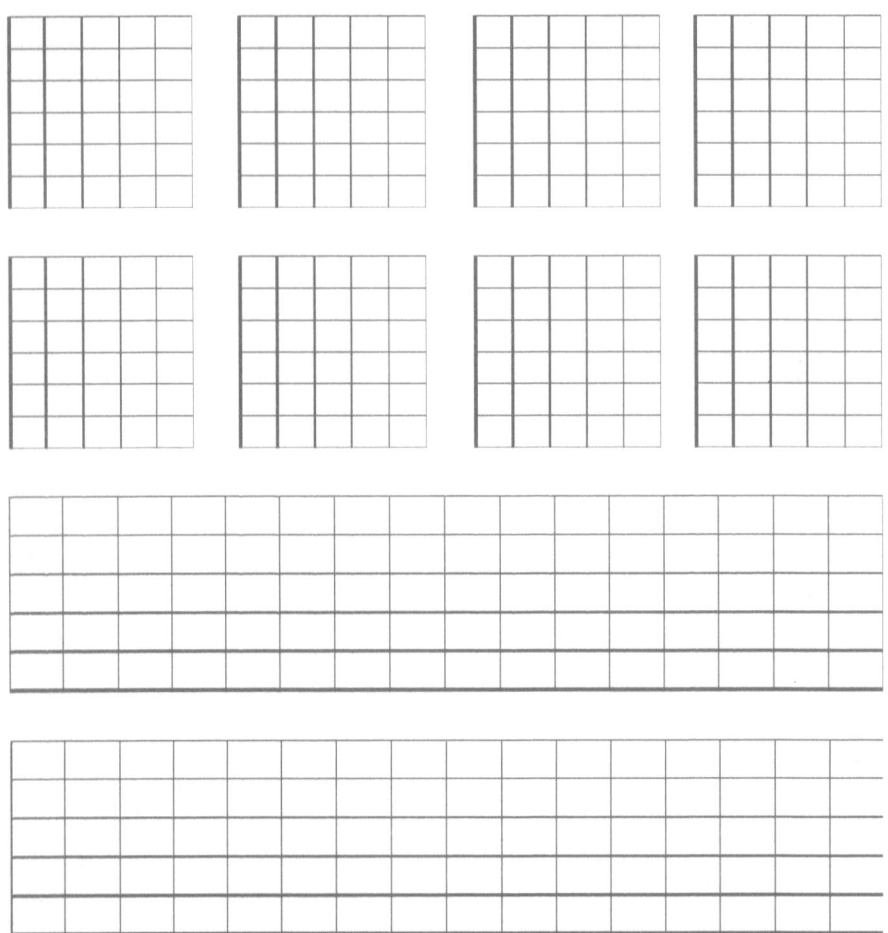

Notes

TAB

TAB

TAB

Date:

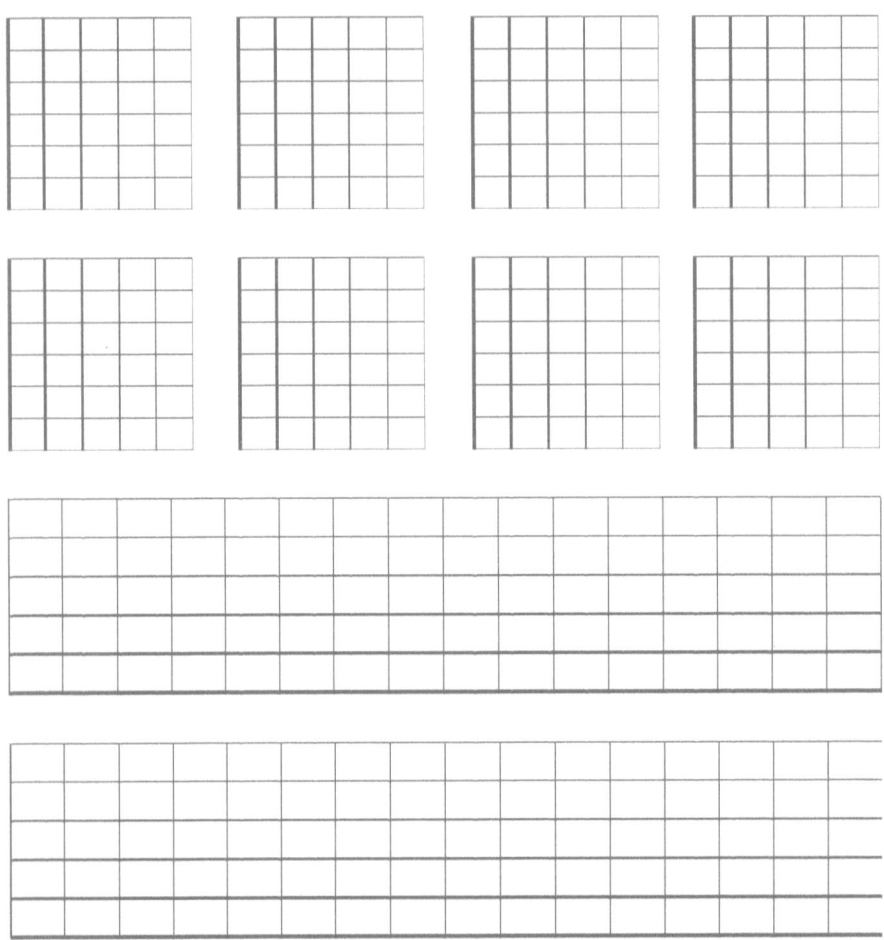

Notes

TAB

TAB

TAB

Date:

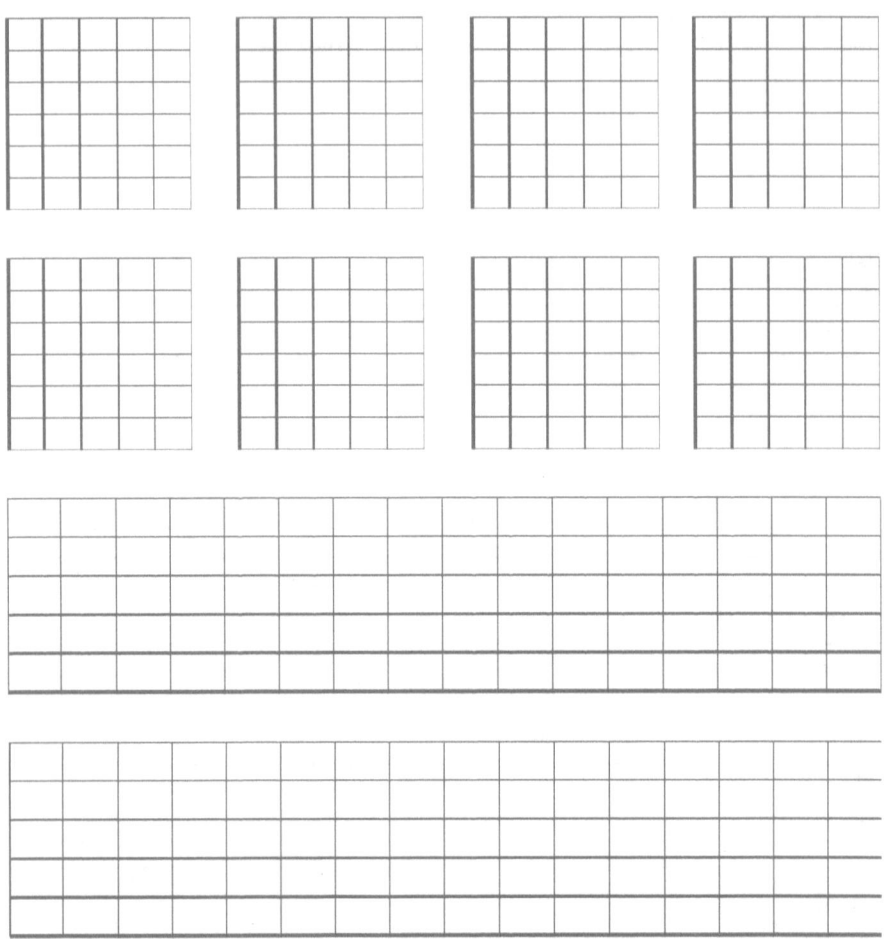

Notes

TAB

TAB

TAB

Date:

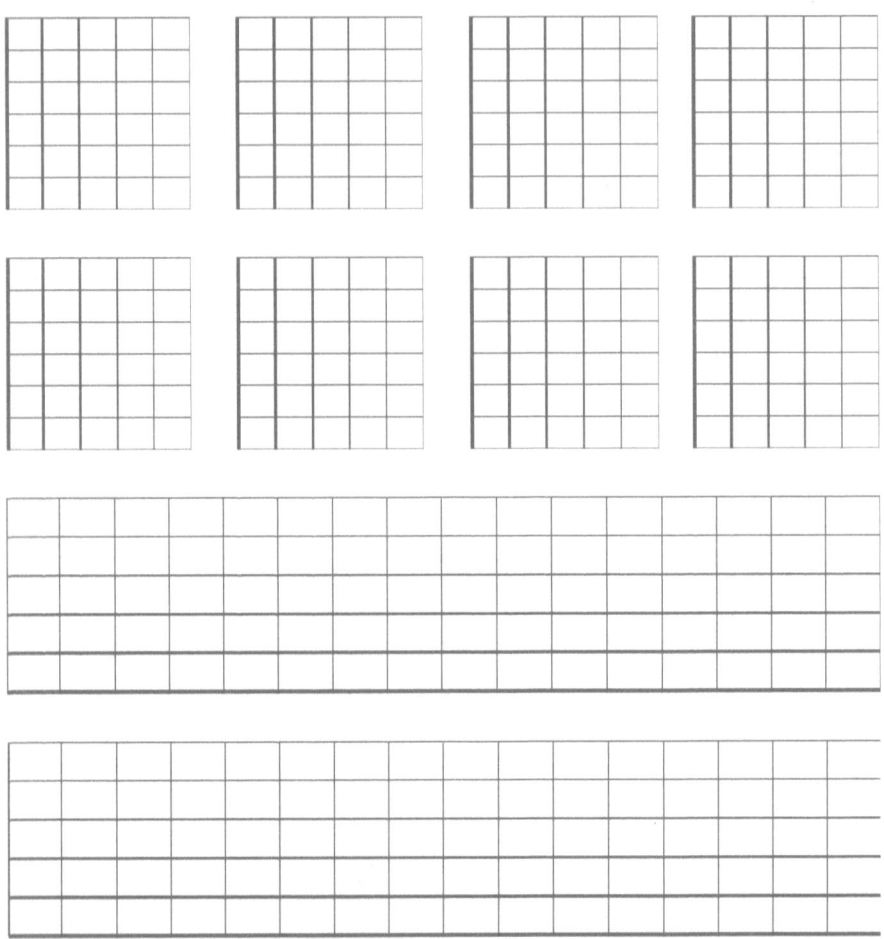

Notes

TAB

TAB

TAB

Date:

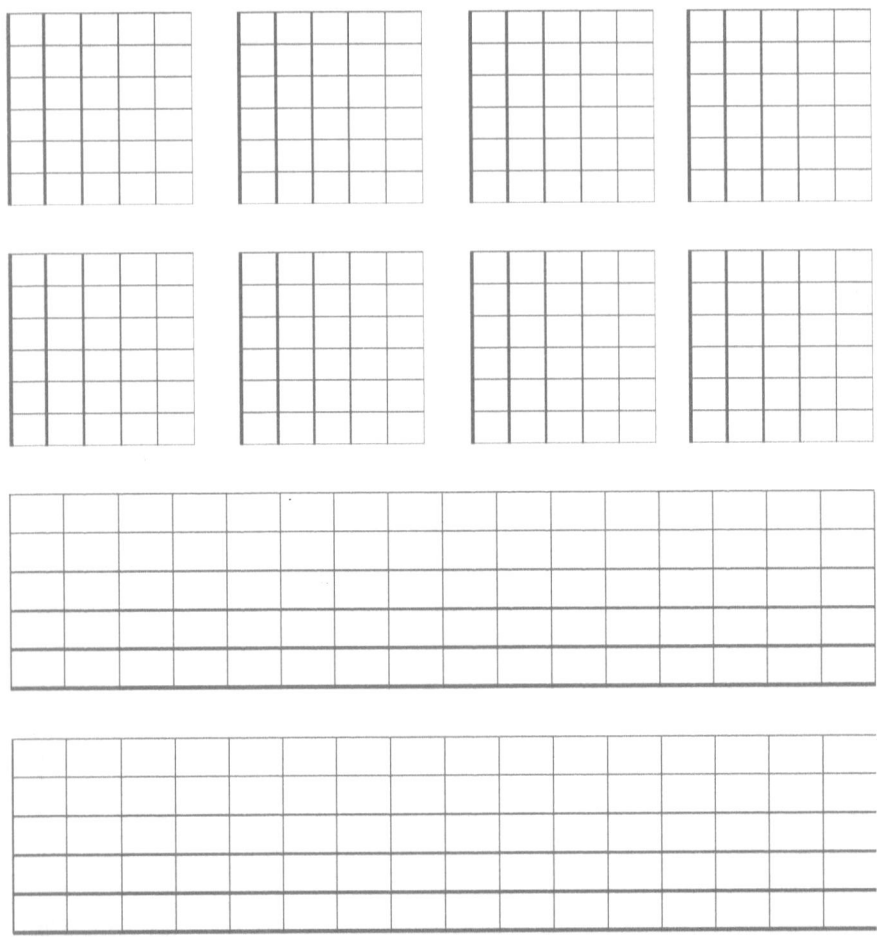

Notes

TAB

TAB

TAB

Date:

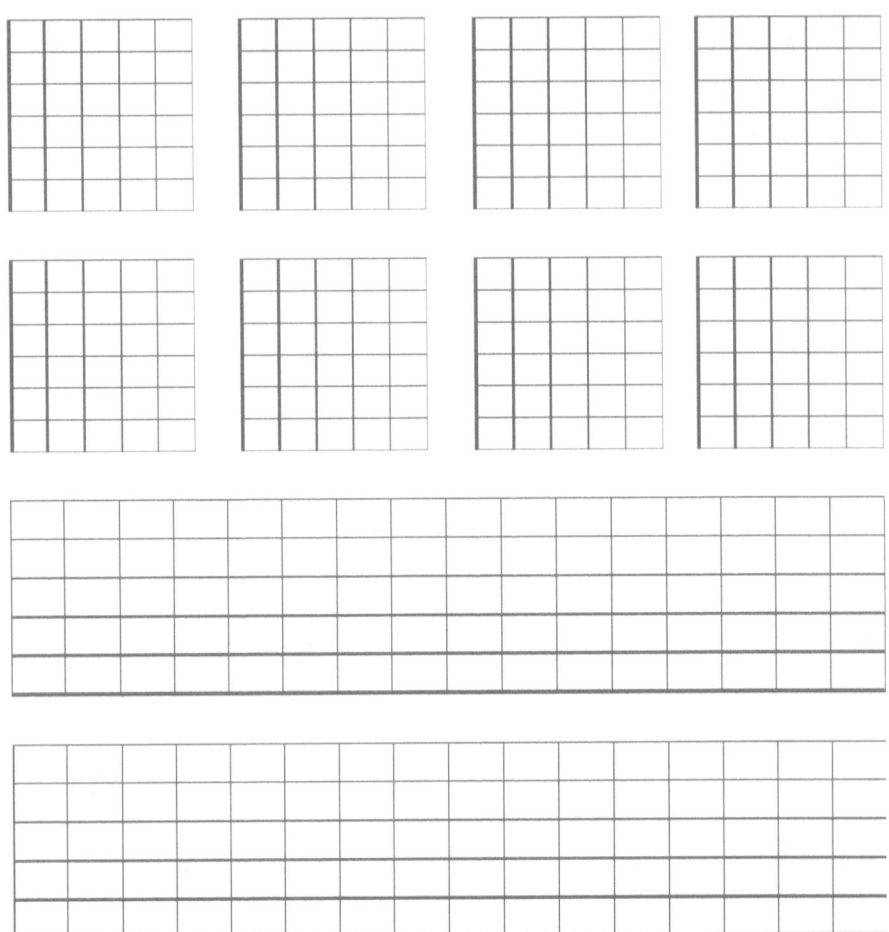

Notes

TAB

TAB

TAB